A COMPLETE GUIDE TO PRESIDENTIAL SEARCH FOR UNIVERSITIES AND COLLEGES

Joseph S. Johnston, Jr.
and
James P. Ferrare

D1262460

AGB
PRESS

1133 20th Street, N.W., Suite 300, Washington, DC 20036
202/296-8400; F 202/223-7053; *www.agb.org*

Since 1921, the Association of Governing Boards of Universities and Colleges (AGB) has had one mission: to strengthen and protect this country's unique form of institutional governance through its research, services, and advocacy. Serving more than 1,250 member boards, nearly 2,000 institutions, and 38,000 individuals, AGB is the only national organization providing university and college presidents, board chairs, trustees, and board professionals of both public and private institutions and institutionally related foundations with resources that enhance their effectiveness.

In accordance with its mission, AGB has developed programs and services that strengthen the partnership between the president and governing board; provide guidance to regents and trustees; identify issues that affect tomorrow's decision making; and foster cooperation among all constituencies in higher education.

For more information, visit *www.agb.org*.

Printed and bound in the United States of America.

A COMPLETE GUIDE TO PRESIDENTIAL SEARCH FOR UNIVERSITIES AND COLLEGES

Copyright © 2013 by AGB Press and the Association of Governing Boards of Universities and Colleges

Library of Congress Control Number: 2013004525

ISBN 978-0-926508-70-5 (alk. paper)

For more information on AGB Press publications or to order additional copies of this book, call (800) 356-6317 or visit the AGB website at *www.agb.org/publications*.

The authors gratefully acknowledge the work of a number of individuals whose writings on presidential search and related topics have been published over the years by AGB in *Trusteeship* magazine and other venues. Although this body of work is, by and large, not cited in the footnotes, *A Complete Guide* draws on the thoughts and words of the following authors and owes much to them: Bruce Alton, Richard Artman, Robert Atwell, Gerald Baliles, Rita Bornstein, Kathleen Lis Dean, Robert Duelks, Mark Franz, William Funk, Carol Guardo, Thomas Ingram, Rachel Levinson-Waldman, Terrence MacTaggart, Theodore Marchese, James Martin, Richard Morrill, Robert O'Neil, Robert Perry, James Samels, William Shelton, James LeRoy Smith, William Weary, and Barbara Wilson. We are also indebted to Thomas Hyatt for his advice.

Finally, we thank the able editorial team of Marla Bobowick, Ellen Hirzy, and Susan Goewey for their many contributions to this project and AGB for the opportunity to undertake it.

Contents

Foreword

> **❝Higher education is in the midst of appropriately disruptive thinking and change.❞**

A*Complete Guide to Presidential Search for Universities and Colleges* presents the essential elements of a presidential search in the context of the current challenges and opportunities confronting colleges, universities, and systems. This is the third volume on the selection of institutional leadership that has its roots in the work of the Association of Governing Boards of Universities and Colleges. This new publication by Joe Johnston and Jamie Ferrare builds on the earlier work of John Nason, a former university president and an early contributor to the study of board governance, in *Presidential Search*, published in 1980 and its revision by Charles Neff and Barbara Leondar in 1992.

In many ways the search and selection process has not changed all that much, but the environment and challenges confronting institution leadership have added a level of complexity to the overall process. In meeting, perhaps, its most essential responsibility, a governing board must commit to a thoughtful, well-designed process that will find a strong and effective leader who understands where higher education is today and where it is going tomorrow, who will provide vision and guidance, who understands the demands of the modern higher education chief executive, and who can work with and mobilize appropriate board and stakeholder engagement in addressing some complex issues.

> **"We need to continue to develop future leaders and find and select those who can meet the calls for change and so much more."**

A Complete Guide outlines a process designed to recruit a high quality pool of candidates—men and women, persons of color and ethnic diversity, regardless of sexual orientation, from traditional and non-traditional backgrounds—who reflect the realities of the next generation of students. Ultimately, the board must lead the way in answering the question, "Who is the *most* qualified person to lead this institution into the future?"

While many board members are experienced in corporate leadership searches, as higher education board members, they need to understand the nuances of a more transparent and inclusive process. A board-designated search committee—consisting of a representative group of institutional and external leaders—recruits, interviews, and recommends candidates to the full board for consideration and selection. To do this work well (and efficiently), professional guidance—in the form of an outside search firm—is a very appropriate investment. It facilitates the search process and allows those making the hard decisions to focus more on the choice than the logistics that can overwhelm the overall effort.

As Joe and Jamie remind us, the board must retain ultimate responsibility for and ownership of the process. They frame a presidential search in the context of a leadership transition that begins with recognition of the departing president and concludes with an onboarding process that extends months beyond the new president's first day in office. These two book-ends of the transition are as much the responsibility of the board as the search itself. Done well, they help to ensure a greater likelihood of success.

In developing *A Complete Guide to Presidential Search for Universities and Colleges*, the authors benefitted from the input of experts who generously shared their perspectives. The practices presented in this book draw on the firsthand expertise of AGB Search consultants and staff, including Tom Courtice, Julie Manus, Ted Marchese, Garry Owens, Oscar Page, Robert Parilla, Ron Stead, Saundra Tracy, and Tobie van der Vorm. We are indebted to them for their thoughtful assistance.

Higher education is in the midst of appropriately disruptive thinking and change. Throughout the sector, we need to continue to develop future leaders and find and select those who can meet the calls for change and so much more. The board's task of selecting a new president comes with a certain amount of risk, but it is also ripe with the possibility for renewal. It is a significant step into the future and one of those responsibilities that, while shared, leads to the making of a decision that a board cannot delegate. The most successful governing bodies will use these moments of leadership transition to learn— not just about potential candidates and campus stakeholders, but also about effective board governance and new directions in higher education.

Richard D. Legon
President
Association of Governing Boards of Universities and Colleges
March 2013

Introduction

> **❝A president comes to personify an institution and shape its future.❞**

FEW MOMENTS HAVE MORE CONSEQUENCE to a college or university than the selection of a new president. More than other leaders, a president comes to personify an institution and shape its future. A president must provide leadership in maintaining and strengthening academic integrity and reputation. He or she must build a sense of shared mission, ensure effective, competitive programs, and secure external support. A good choice can benefit a college or university far into the future. A poor one can exact a heavy and lasting toll. The process of presidential search and selection carries both enormous opportunity and considerable risk. It is crucial to get it right.

THE BOARD RESPONSIBILITY

In American higher education, the legal responsibility for selecting a president is borne solely by governing boards. All boards, by law, hold their institutions in trust. The Association of Governing Boards of Universities and Colleges (AGB) identifies a set of basic obligations that boards must discharge in their legal roles as fiduciaries. Board members are involved, for example, in establishing the institution's mission and approving its strategic plan, ensuring fiscal integrity and academic quality, and preserving institutional autonomy and academic freedom. But two of the board's paramount responsibilities focus squarely on the chief executive. The board selects and appoints the individual to serve in this position and then assesses his or her performance. In many ways, a presidential search is the most important task a governing board undertakes.

The responsibility of selecting a president is one role boards face often. Recent data suggest that they will need to face it more and more frequently. Every year for some years, 400 to 500 presidencies have changed,[1] a figure consistent with estimates that between one-fourth and one-third of accredited colleges and universities are either preparing for or engaged in presidential searches each year.[2] Today's presidents are older, but they are serving notably shorter tenures, an average of 7 years in 2011, down from 8.5 years in 2006.[3] Age and increasing job turnover spell the likelihood that colleges and universities will lose their presidents more frequently to retirement or other causes in the coming years. Boards, in turn, will need to find their successors.

WHO SHOULD READ THIS BOOK

Although boards reserve the final decision about presidential selection, it is extremely rare these days for an entire board to conduct the search that produces the final candidates. Instead, most create a search committee and charge it with screening candidates. In addition to appointing a majority of the committee members from the board, most also include selected members of the college or university community— often faculty, staff, alumni, students, and other significant stakeholders. This group is an ad hoc committee assisted in many cases by a professional search consultant and potentially staffed by someone at the institution. The committee makes recommendations based on its charge from the board, and the board makes a final decision as to the candidate to select.

---

[1] Robert Hastings Perry, "When Times Call for an Interim President," *Trusteeship*, March/April 2003, p. 1.

[2] James E. Samels and James Martin, "Shaky Ground in Troubled Times: The Legal Framework of Presidential Transitions," in James Martin, James E. Samels, and Associates, *Presidential Transition in Higher Education: Managing Leadership Change* (Baltimore: Johns Hopkins University Press, 2004), p. 198.

[3] Center for Policy Analysis, *The American College President 2012* (Washington, DC: American Council on Education, 2012), p. 5.

In this book, we offer guidance to those who have a role in presidential search, selection, and appointment. The audience includes the boards that have ultimate responsibility as well as board members who may be planning for leadership transitions. It also includes search committees and transition groups to which boards delegate, under their oversight, so much of the work entailed when a vacancy does occur. Another audience is the members of a college or university staff—especially board professionals and general counsel—who support the process in a variety of important ways.

Although we refer primarily to campus searches, the discussion largely applies to searches for system heads as well. See pages 60–61 and 122 for a brief summary of how state boards of regents (or governors, or the equivalent) typically conduct such efforts.

The intended audience, finally, includes those institutions that choose to use a search firm or consultant and those that do not. These days, a large and growing majority use consultants. And for reasons to be explained in Chapter 4, they are following best practice. All those contemplating or engaged in a presidential search—whether with professional assistance or not—should find this book's content of value.

OPPORTUNITIES AND RISKS

Colleges and universities should seize the opportunity presented by moments of transition. At first, these periods might seem daunting and uncertain, but boards, search committees, and entire campus communities often welcome them as occasions for partnership. They use transitions to look closely at their institutions and understand them as changing, developing organizations, perhaps with very different needs from those they had three, five, or ten years before. Then they are able to find leaders whose skills, interests, and backgrounds match evolving realities. These new chief executives in turn are equipped—in increasingly challenging times —to tackle difficult problems, lead change, and open up exciting new possibilities, including some that had been out of reach. Through well-designed, well-executed leadership transitions, they manage to unite and inspire campus constituencies and secure common commitment to new leadership and updated agendas. They—and the searches that brought them to their new positions—have renewed their institutions.

But the business of searching for and selecting presidents can entail sobering risks.

Often, for example, boards may seem uninvolved in searches or, by contrast, act with too strong a hand. They can be accused of being insensitive to constituents' needs and desires and of failing to include them as they should. Outside politics can impinge inappropriately. Confidentiality may be breached, and damaging rumors circulated widely. Those inside and outside of the process—including, on occasion, candidates—can lose trust in the integrity, effectiveness, or fairness of a search. Boards sometimes seem unable to reach consensus on the kind of candidate wanted. The rules and procedures governing the search may come into dispute or be changed midway. Factions can form behind individual candidates, distracting the community, undercutting morale, and possibly hastening the departure of valued staff. Controversy surrounding the search may find its way into the media, causing widespread disaffection among alumni, friends, and the public and damaging the institution's good name. Deliberations can seem rushed and due diligence lacking. The best candidates can fall away. A candidate selected through what is perceived as a flawed search is unduly burdened by the task of winning over skeptical constituents. The shortcomings of someone selected too hastily soon become apparent. Or a search may run aground entirely, failing to produce anyone who can and is willing to be appointed.

Because situations like these do arise, the history of presidential searches is replete with disappointing efforts and a good many abysmal failures. But more common by far are the many instances in which good planning, hard work, and a measure of luck have produced well-accepted and promising outcomes that set institutions on solid footing.

A FOCUS ON BEST PRACTICE

Over the years, AGB has observed and studied the process of presidential search and has developed an understanding of the basic approaches and specific steps that are most likely to produce good results. No single, perfect method exists for every institution. Many variations among searches are appropriate and necessary given differences in institutional type or culture, resources available, and types of candidates sought. This diversity, however, makes the broad outlines of good practice all the more clear. Again and again, effective searches are marked by certain values, goals, strategies, and tactics. Just as reliably, searches that go wrong—that lose people's confidence, say, or result in the appointment of someone ill-suited to the job—have their commonalities. For this reason, this book focuses on best practice. When necessary, it explains the choices presented at a crossroads in the search process or summarizes the advantages and disadvantages of alternative routes. Largely, however, it describes what AGB considers the most proven ways of search and selection. These are the main roads that most boards and search committees will want to travel. Their journey will always be challenging, but with a good sense of how others have managed it successfully, they can undertake it with confidence.

A note on terminology: In the United States, the terms *president* and *chancellor* are used inconsistently. The chief executive officers of independent institutions almost always hold the title of president, but public colleges and university campuses are often led by chancellors. In some states, the title of chancellor is reserved for the person who oversees a multi-campus system, and those who lead the campuses are presidents. Throughout this book, we use the term *president* to refer to all college and university chief executive officers, regardless of their official designations.

Key Points

- **Boards are solely responsible for the selection of presidents.**
  It is in many ways their most important task.

- **Presidencies turn over frequently** and will do so more frequently
  in the future.

- **Presidential searches can unite campuses and inspire them
  to tackle challenges**, make needed changes, and reach for new
  possibilities.

- **Effective searches share certain qualities**—as do ineffective
  ones.

Part

I | A TIME OF CHANGE: BEGINNING THE TRANSITION

1. Establishing a Transition Planning
   Framework

2. Announcing a President's Departure

3. Departing Presidents, Interim
   Leadership, and Internal Candidates

Chapter 1
Establishing a Transition Planning Framework

❝The time for the board's work on transition is always now.❞

PRESIDENTIAL SEARCH IS ONE ELEMENT in a larger process: leadership transition. The board's goal, after all, is not simply to find and appoint a successor to a departing president. It is to bring an institution through a period of change by strengthening it and securing new leadership that has the best possible chance of success. Clearing this higher bar requires the board to be ready well before it learns the news of a departure and to stay engaged through the early months of the new presidency and beyond. Transition planning and management are not one-time events. They involve planning and preparing for leadership change that is linked to the institution's priorities and mission, carrying out a search, and installing, supporting, assessing, and staying in close communication with an incumbent about his or her future. The time for the board's work on transition is always now.

The need for a new leader can develop and come to the board's attention in different ways. Sometimes it results from a well-anticipated retirement, sometimes from a president's moving on to another position with ample notice given. The board itself may take the initiative to terminate or not renew a president, offering and providing an orderly exit. But, on occasion, departures happen unexpectedly. Illness, death, fecklessness, scandal, malfeasance, institutional crisis, serious disagreement—any of these situations can create a sudden vacancy.

PRELIMINARY QUESTIONS

Boards are often stunned by the news of a presidential departure. Caught unprepared, they may be unsure about the necessary first steps and the path forward. Because institutions may be vulnerable to uncertainty and demoralization at these moments—and boards may risk outright missteps—these failures of board leadership can be costly. Boards that have anticipated the various possibilities and worked out at least general and provisional answers to some preliminary questions will be far more likely to know what they need to do and cope effectively.

First, well before they address how to conduct the search, they may ask these questions about the immediate challenges and first steps:

- What guidance is available to us?
- Does the situation on campus need stabilizing? If so, what are its causes, and what steps will improve things?
- Why do we find ourselves in this situation?
- What are our basic responsibilities going forward—our authority, powers, and obligations?
- Do we want to have a search, or should we at least look first at whether there is an outstanding internal candidate ready to assume the presidency?
- Should we move directly into a search for a permanent successor, or do circumstances require a period of interim leadership?
- What and how should we communicate now with the community and public?

Next, if the search and appointment process hasn't been planned, it will need to be debated and designed using these guiding questions:

- Who takes what role? With what guidance and support?
- How do we communicate with the campus and with the community?
- Will we assess the institution's needs, challenges, and opportunities before we begin the search?
- How will our search committee be constituted, and who will lead it?

- Where will we find good search consultants, and how do we select among them?
- How long should a search take?
- Where will the resources come from?
- How many candidates do we want the search committee to recommend to the board? Will we want them ranked or unranked?
- What kind of contract terms should we be prepared to offer?
- How can we ensure that the community unites around the selected individual?

A prudent board will also anticipate the ongoing communications challenges posed by a transition and the sitting president's role through such a period. Planning extends to difficult but necessary actions that may best be taken at such a time of change, actions for which the board would not want its new president held accountable. And it will provide a roadmap to the launch of the new executive's tenure, outlining the steps that ensure he or she is effective and well supported.

ORGANIZING FOR ONGOING TRANSITION PLANNING

It makes sense to establish broad procedures for presidential transitions so that they are in place before an actual search is necessary. Probably the most frequent approach is to charge the executive committee with this responsibility and ask it to report its recommendations to the full board. Executive committees tend to oversee annual presidential performance reviews and, if there is no separate compensation committee, employment contracts as well. These activities are the locus of most conversation and negotiation with an incumbent about his or her future, and so executive committees are especially well positioned to understand and influence how a president sees the months and years to come.

Another approach is to form a separate transition committee, ideally at the outset of a new presidency. In a public college or university setting, open meeting and open record laws may determine how such a group may be appointed and do its work.[4] As an operating committee of the board, the transition committee develops written guidance,

---

[4] William E. Weary, "The Role of the Board in Presidential Transition," in Martin and Samels, *Presidential Transition*, p. 62.

> **" The full board should ensure that the current president fully understands, supports, and contributes to transition planning. "**

approved by the board, for the next transition and for ongoing monitoring of all matters related to leadership planning and change, from resignation to inauguration.

Even if no entity is formed or no existing one charged with primary responsibility, there's a *function* that should be provided for. Formal board policies (such as a presidential succession plan) should anticipate how a presidential search would be handled. Such policies should spell out, for example, whether a search firm should be used and how the search committee should be constituted. Also, as part of its yearly review of a president, the executive committee should discuss succession plans and grooming, if appropriate, of internal candidates. Although there may be little current work to do beyond that, the committee should be ready to go into action should a president resign or give the board other reason for concern.

The full board should ensure that the current president fully understands, supports, and contributes to transition planning. Launching this process at the outset of a presidency may help in this regard. But where there is no process, the case is strong for initiating it regardless of where a president is in his or her tenure. A decision to start transition planning in no way reflects on an incumbent. Like getting one's financial and personal effects in order, anticipating what will need to be done when the inevitable departure takes place is simple good sense and responsible practice.

Key Points

- **An effective board focuses continually on renewing the institution** and strengthening its leadership capacity.

- **When a president departs, the board should first address basic questions** about the current campus situation, whether to proceed with a search, and how to communicate with the community and public.

- **The board's own prior transition planning will help** with the many decisions to be made.

Additional Articles from *Trusteeship*

Bornstein, Rita. "Succession Planning: The Time Has Come." *Trusteeship* (September/October 2010): p. 28.

Ferrare, James P. and Theodore J. Marchese. "Increasing the Odds for Successful Presidential Searches." *Trusteeship* (September/October 2010): p. 24.

Funk, R. William. "A Presidential Search Is Opportunity Knocking." *Trusteeship* (September/October 2005): p. 18.

Lapovsky, Lucie. "The Best-Laid Succession Plans." *Trusteeship* (January/February 2006): p. 20.

For more recommended reading, see Resources at the end of this book.

Chapter 2

Announcing a President's Departure

> **❝The board's most important goal… should be to inspire confidence among all stakeholders.❞**

THE NEWS OF A PRESIDENT'S DEPARTURE—whether it is long anticipated or a total surprise—tends to provoke strong feelings. As members of the campus community contemplate changes to the familiar order, they may feel insecure, if not fearful or distressed. A popular president's leaving may cause real sadness. Relief, or even elation, may be the reaction in other cases. Even when reactions are more muted or mixed, people usually recognize that big changes may soon be afoot that could affect everyone. Yet no one knows what those changes might be. Few understand how a new president will be selected. Speculation often abounds, both on and off campus. Rumors fill any vacuum of information. In the absence of effective board leadership, apprehensions can take hold, key relationships can become frayed, and valuable staff may quickly begin to look elsewhere.

Although a growing number of governing boards have transition planning in place, in reality, that guidance is necessarily general and provisional. Transition plans, which are human products outlining hypothetical practices, can only imperfectly anticipate the often testing realities that the board and an institution will confront. But this much is certain: Whether it has done transition planning or not, and whether a president's departure has been expected or not, the board needs to plan and carry out a strategic series of announcements and other communications during the challenging early hours and days of a transition. These activities include:

- Reviewing institutional policies for search and transition guidance;
- Carrying out a well-conceived strategy to notify key stakeholders, the campus community, and the public;
- Determining the content and logistics of the announcement;
- Addressing issues related to an unplanned departure; and
- Acknowledging the departing leader's accomplishments.

IMMEDIATE STEPS

In the earliest hours of a transition, the board's leadership will want to confirm the bounds of its authority and review institutional policies that may require certain actions or provide guidance. It should consult the college or university counsel in reviewing relevant passages in bylaws, codes, and state regulations. System regulations may constrain public institutions significantly. In fact, in a number of states the system's board and staff handle centrally all matters relating to the appointment and service of a president (including the search).

In most cases, the departing president continues in office until a successor is identified and appointed. When a vacancy is sudden, however, a predetermined emergency succession plan may need to take effect, even if it is temporary. Longer-term interim appointments are addressed in Chapter 3.

ANNOUNCEMENT STRATEGY

The board's most important goal when announcing a presidential departure should be to inspire confidence among all stakeholders. Both internal and external communities need to know that the board is moving deliberately and strategically to ensure a seamless and successful leadership transition. The announcement should always come from the board and president first, not from other sources, so that it can shape public reception. Except where there is serious controversy, bad feeling, or estrangement, the board's leadership should involve the departing president and the vice president for communications (or other chief communications staff member) in planning the timing, content, and other details of the announcement. Three separate announcements should be made in sequence: first to key stakeholders, then to the internal campus community, and finally to the public.

The ways and means of the announcement will vary. One president, for example, announced her own retirement in a public statement, accompanied by the board chair's thanks for her dedication and service to the university. It is also appropriate for faculty and student leaders to issue a statement of support and thanks. Another board explained the reasons for a president's involuntary departure as "philosophical differences," with no further detail. Depending on the circumstances, other institutions may be more transparent about their motives for dismissing a president or asking for his or her resignation.

The board's leadership should reach out immediately to those who should hear the news before it is made known in a large-group or public announcement. Once a decision has been communicated to or from a president, board chair, and/or system head or other controlling government authority, these individuals should be apprised, more or less in this order:

- Key state policy leaders (in a public institution);
- Board members;
- Executive staff;
- Key donors;
- Faculty, student, and alumni leaders; and
- Significant friends and partners of the institution.

Face-to-face meetings or personal phone calls are appropriate and appreciated. If the president's departure is planned, he or she may wish to inform some of these parties personally. For those in positions of authority at the institution, early notice is essential so they can assume responsibility for their roles in an effective transition. For key outside individuals, it is more than a courtesy to inform them early. Not only can the board prevent ruffled feelings or serious offense, it sends a message that the recipients and those they represent are highly valued by the institution and part of an inner circle whose support is counted on at critical moments.

Usually the president and board chair together will make the internal announcement to the campus community. Faculty and staff should never hear the news first from
the media. Whether the communication occurs in a special all-campus meeting or
through a hand-distributed memorandum or email depends in part on such factors as
institutional size, complexity, and culture. The campus announcement should take place
no more than a few hours before the first public announcement in order to minimize
leaks and less-than-accurate reporting. Alumni should be apprised as soon as possible
through electronic and regularly scheduled print communications.

ANNOUNCEMENT LOGISTICS AND CONTENT

The institution's vice president for communications leads the effort to craft the campus
and public announcements and related communications, which will include appropriate media releases, radio and television announcements, web and social media postings,
and the like. A small group of board and staff members who are closely responsible for
the transition should consult on the content and develop a set of talking points for the announcement. The participants usually include the departing president, the board chair
(and possibly the chairs of the board's transition and search committees), and legal counsel. In some cases, when the circumstances are problematic, the group may want to agree
to follow the talking points scrupulously, avoiding editorial comment, speculation, and
any other improvisation. At such times, one person—usually the board chair—should
serve as the single public spokesperson to make the announcement and, with support
from the group, answer all inquiries.

Usually the campus and public announcements simply summarize the circumstances, acknowledge the departing president's service (with some information as to his
or her future plans), and preview plans for finding new leadership. In a happy transition
that has allowed time for planning, more expansiveness is appropriate. A difficult departure, especially if it is sudden, will probably require more discipline. In either case, tone
can be as important as content, and it should be personal and reassuring, appreciative
and optimistic. All concerned will want to feel that, whether the tenure has been successful or troubled, the institution is strong and its leaders are engaged.[5]

---

[5] See John Ross, "Leaks Kill: Communication and Presidential Transition," in Martin and Samels,
Presidential Transition, pp. 178–81.

The announcement should deal with search plans only to the degree that the board's unrushed deliberations to this point can support them. If the president's decision has been handled in a discreet, collaborative, and relaxed fashion, and if an ongoing transition planning process has been in place, the board probably will

> 66 **Usually the president and board chair together will make the internal announcement to the campus community.** 99

have had time to decide on details such as the scope of the search, the composition of the search committee, and the time it will take to find a successor. But events may have so outpaced planning that the board's leadership needs to wait until after the announcement to make these decisions. The announcement will serve to reassure internal and external communities that there is a process directed by an able and committed board and that decisions will be made promptly and communicated in full.

ACKNOWLEDGING THE PRESIDENT'S ACHIEVEMENTS

The announcement will be the first of many opportunities to acknowledge publicly the hard work and achievements of the departing institutional leader and his or her spouse or partner. Most presidents at the end of their tenure deserve deep respect and gratitude, and the community will want to see them thanked and honored. Matters were well handled, for example, when the president of one research university stepped down after 20 years of service and a successful search for his successor. Key constituencies released statements thanking the president, and the president-elect issued public congratulations to his predecessor for his years of dedication and leadership. In the week before the president's departure, the board hosted a dinner in his honor and announced that they had raised funds for a scholarship bearing his name.

Even with a president who has been less than successful or has been terminated, it is best to take a high road in all matters, including that of public praise. No one will be well-served by a chilly silence toward a departing incumbent or, of course, the slightest airing of dirty linen; the institution's ability to attract a new president might well be the first victim. It is best to find contributions for which the incumbent can be commended and thanked and to present a campus community that is united and looking forward.

WHEN A DEPARTURE IS UNPLANNED

Fortunately, most presidents serve competently and honestly, give ample notice of their departure, and leave no severe problems in their wake. But with an unplanned departure, there will be little time for the board to probe into any serious financial, personnel, or other issues that may come to light before an initial announcement. In that situation, the board's leadership should make every effort in the time available to determine the nature and extent of any issues that are discovered. It should choose carefully among the options so that, if necessary, the outlines of a plan for fuller investigation and resolution can be shared as part of the announcement.

When there is an unhappy parting of the ways, the board will want to seek legal advice on terms of separation and confirm its obligations to the departing leader and vice versa. It may want to secure organizational property and protect access to computer and financial accounts. Assisted by legal counsel, the board may seek a written agreement that, among other tenets, firmly prohibits either party's disparaging the other. The institution's human resources office should also be appropriately engaged as personnel-related issues are worked through.

When those who shepherd institutions through the earliest hours of an institutional transition are sensitive to these kinds of considerations and take these kinds of measures, they are likely to avoid serious mistakes and save themselves any number of problems. They will continue to be under pressure to make numerous decisions quickly, but they will clear the way to a stage where they can engage in somewhat more systematic planning—measured typically in days rather than hours. This is critical, as whatever has not been thought through and settled in prior transition planning will need to be taken up next.

Key Points

- **The board's leaders should be visible**, fully engaged, and reassuring as the news of the president's departure becomes public.

- **For key constituencies, provide basic information**, identify next steps, and project confidence about the future.

- **Most presidents deserve to be honored at the end of their tenure.** Take time to decide how to thank the president and his or her spouse or partner.

Additional Articles from *Trusteeship*

Footlick, Jerrold K. "A Steady Hand During a Presidential Crisis." *Trusteeship* (September/October 2000): pp. 15 – 19.

Marchese, Theodore J. "Making the Most of Presidential Transitions." *Trusteeship* (January/February 2012): p. 25.

Pierce, Susan Resneck. "Toward a Smooth Presidential Transition." *Trusteeship* (September/October 2003): pp. 13 – 17.

For more recommended reading, see Resources at the end of this book.

Chapter 3
Departing Presidents, Interim Leadership, and Internal Candidates

❝Transitions do not always proceed according to a prescribed formula.❞

I n most leadership transitions, the announcement of a president's leaving or intention to leave leads more or less directly to a broad, public search for a permanent successor. The president usually remains in office until a successor is appointed. But transitions do not always proceed according to a prescribed formula. To ensure a process that fits the needs of the university, college, or system, the board may need to consider three questions immediately after the announcement and before launching the search:

- How will the departing president be involved, if at all, in the search and transition?
- Should the board appoint an acting or interim president?
- Should the search be open to internal candidates?

DEPARTING PRESIDENTS

Even more than most variables in institutional transitions, the role of the outgoing president during and after the announcement of his or her departure depends on a variety of circumstances. Has the president decided to retire in full consultation with the board? Accepted another position elsewhere? Been involuntarily terminated? Does his or her contract—as it should—anticipate certain arrangements, carefully thought through by the board? If so, do these include a faculty position? Is he or she highly regarded and able to be helpful in areas like fundraising? What are the preferences of his or her successor likely to be?

If a respected and valued president is retiring, the board may encourage selected types of continuing involvement, subject to guidelines and common sense. But if distrust or hard feelings exist, it is best to look for ways to minimize, if not sever, the relationship. Many presidencies end equivocally, with mixed emotions on all sides. In this situation, too, although the departing leader can sometimes be kept engaged in useful ways and without much risk, caution and limits are in order.

INVOLVING THE DEPARTING PRESIDENT

Purposeful involvement. Thinking back on his presidency, one retiring president knew he would have benefited at the beginning from the firsthand reflections of his predecessor on fundamental campus issues. He had enough lead time, so he decided to ease the transition for his successor by keeping a working journal during his last year. He created a month-by-month record of activities and decisions in key areas— such as admissions, budget, and ongoing projects—along with projections of whether similar issues might need to be addressed in the first year. But he was clear that his journal was not the place to document personal activities, make recommendations, or offer long-term solutions. Written in the voice of an experienced predecessor, his journal helped the new president know what to expect.

A cautionary tale. A retiring president with an admitted penchant for controlling things immediately contacted her successor to suggest meetings, conferences, and issues that he needed to deal with during the transition and before taking office. Without a sense of priorities or knowledge of campus personnel, the president-elect quickly felt conflicted and confused. The board responded immediately by appointing a transition committee, with members representing a variety of constituencies and a board member as chair. All communications with the new president—including those from the retiring president—went through this committee. The board avoided a conflict between predecessor and successor, managed transition issues successfully, and enabled the president-elect to finish his last six months at his current institution without interruption.

A president who remains in place until a successor is named might have a special set of responsibilities—completion of certain projects, for example, or a capital campaign. Having specific assignments can lessen the chances that he or she will be seen as a lame duck, a perception that often causes a loss of institutional momentum. Such a president may also be helpful to the search and transition committees. Although participation in interviews is not appropriate, he or she might: provide contacts with possible nominators and references; be available, if requested, to meet with and answer questions from finalists; and help plan the new appointee's orientation.

In some institutional settings and with some individuals, it may make sense for the former president to be kept involved professionally. Departing presidents can often be very helpful by introducing their successors to key donors or business partners. Occasionally they join the faculty, head up university foundations, or even assume the title and largely ceremonial duties of chancellor. Some are given certain kinds of support, such as an office or clerical help, without portfolio. And others are retained as consultants. If the former president is not moving away, however, it is often in everyone's interest that he or she take at least a short sabbatical before returning.

Any relationship—except for service on the faculty—should be subject to the approval and control of the new president. Some argue that the departing president should not continue to live in the area or return often to visit. Temptations and opportunities to opine on the successor's work may be too frequent otherwise. Wherever departing presidents live and whatever professional roles they move into, their golden rule is to be available and offer help, but only if their successor asks. After years in their positions, most departing presidents understand this rule and have the grace and good sense to embrace it. Those few who do not might need to be gently reminded.

ACTING AND INTERIM PRESIDENCIES

From time to time, boards appoint temporary leadership, either acting or interim. They might choose this option for a number of reasons:

- To stabilize a difficult campus situation or resolve difficult issues;
- To provide leadership when the departing president wants or needs to leave before a successor is found;

- To set the stage for a successor by taking corrective actions or completing projects;
- To maintain institutional momentum until a new president is selected; and
- To fill the gap when a search needs to be reopened.

The board may or may not postpone a search during the acting or interim leadership period.

Some use the terms *acting* and *interim* interchangeably, and others distinguish carefully between them. An *acting president* generally comes from inside the institution—an executive vice president, vice president of academic affairs, or dean, for example. He or she serves for a relatively short period—for instance, up to six months, or until the search concludes—and receives increased compensation for the duration. At a minimum, boards look to an acting president for sustained, competent management. An *interim president* can come from either inside or, more often, outside an institution and can serve for six months to a year or more. He or she is more likely to have served as a president elsewhere, to have been chosen for a particular expertise, or both. Some search firms now offer as a service help in finding interim candidates who are well matched to an institution's short-term needs.

Sometimes the board seeks acting or interim leadership when the campus is in turmoil, perhaps associated with the president's stepping down. The board decides that its top priority is to stabilize the situation quickly and give all parties some time and breathing room. Or the board may sense that the campus, while calm, is not ready for a search until some troublesome problems are resolved or key issues are decided. There may be, for example, infighting among executive staff, or financial controls may be inadequate.

A temporary leader, especially one with long experience and relative independence (and thus the ability to be candid), can help the board see its situation more clearly. He or she can tackle thorny problems that might threaten a new permanent presidency if they are not confronted and resolved immediately. The board can also use his or her tenure to undertake corrective actions or initiatives that it doesn't want to lay at a new president's feet. Classic examples are the reassignment or termination of underperforming staff or the costly but needed renovation of the president's house. Whatever the case, a temporary leader can often clear the way and set the stage advantageously for a permanent successor. The board should have a full list of major issues for the interim president to address before the new president takes over.

> **❝ Certain traits will be desired of anyone in the interim position—integrity, breadth of experience, professional temperament, high levels of energy—other expectations should relate directly to the challenges the college is expected to face and overcome in the near future.❞**

Boards should be careful when defining their expectations of interim or acting presidencies. While certain traits will be desired of anyone in the position—including integrity, breadth of experience, professional temperament, and high levels of energy—other expectations should relate directly to the challenges the college or university is expected to face and overcome in the near future. The skills of a fundraiser may be needed to lead a comprehensive campaign to a successful conclusion. A business strategist will be able to address the problems of a business model under pressure. Or a diplomat could mediate disagreements and bring warring parts of the campus community together. Beyond these specific expectations, the board should reach an explicit understanding with the interim president about the kinds of contributions and leadership it does and doesn't want. Absolute candor in the interim's assessment of the institution? Probably yes. But a transformational leadership style? A role and/or a voice in identifying, vetting, cultivating, and selecting a permanent president? Possibly an ex officio seat on the search committee? Sometimes one of more of these contributions or qualities will be welcome, but sometimes they go a step too far. Especially since an interim president typically is given more authority than an acting one, it will also be wise to discuss where he or she must stop short of making preemptive choices that rightly belong to the new president.

Whatever the interim's responsibilities may be, the board should introduce and treat him or her as a chief executive. This attitude is vital, especially if the board is asking this leader to tackle hard problems. If he or she is perceived as a caretaker, little will be accomplished. Faculty and staff may attempt end runs around the interim president to board members or others who are seen as having the real power.

Finally, the board should be clear whether it wants to allow an acting or interim president to be a candidate for the permanent position. Sometimes an acting or interim is appointed with the thought (shared or not) that the period of temporary leadership will allow everyone to see how he or she might do in the job. And there may be an understandable reluctance to rule out any such internal candidate in the event that the board will regret eliminating this person too early if circumstances change and he or she looks better later.[6] Strong arguments are made on the other side of this issue, however. Acting and interim presidents, many have said, are prone to conflicts of interest, or at least set up for awkward decision making, if they are also candidates.

INTERNAL CANDIDATES

Should internal candidates be permitted in the search for a new president? The board's policy on this matter should be decided before a search is launched or a search firm retained. The decision is the board's to make, and the question can be a difficult one. The existence of a strong inside candidate, especially one that is the acting or interim president, may suggest to some that a search is "wired." As a result, outside candidates may be reluctant to be considered, and the pool will not be as robust as it could or should be. The board may therefore want to resist the temptation, say, to encourage the candidacy of an acting president chosen from inside the institution because he or she "deserves a chance," unless the individual is thought to be highly competitive as well. But in some situations, a temporary leader or other internal candidate might be truly compelling, while an honest search instead of a direct appointment is thought to be important as well. The board may believe that if such valued individuals are not allowed to compete for the position, or are not chosen for it, they will be likely to leave the institution. In such cases, the board may decide that it can accept the possibility of a somewhat less impressive pool, reasoning that losing the internal candidate could turn out to be more costly.

If the board does decide to allow or even pursue internal candidates, it should be vigilant in ensuring that, as much as possible, they receive the same treatment as those applying from outside. It requires a certain suspension of disbelief on the part of search committee members to interview someone they know well in the same manner as they

---

[6] See Jean A. Dowdall, *Searching for Higher Education Leadership: Advice for Candidates and Search Committees* (Lanham, MD: Rowman & Littlefield, 2007), pp. 70–71.

DIRECT APPOINTMENT WITHOUT A SEARCH

Boards sometimes appoint a new president without conducting a formal national search. Three circumstances might prompt the board to take this route:

1. **A small, denominational institution** requires a president from a particular religious order and identifies a suitable candidate through existing networks.

2. **A natural successor from inside or outside** is well known to and highly regarded by the board and campus community and is enthusiastic about becoming president.

3. **Internal succession planning and leadership development** advance a strong candidate from the faculty or administrative staff.

The second and third approaches may be the most common. A study by the American Council on Education shows that one in three current presidents have been inside hires.[7] At its best, hiring from inside honors the institution's staff, establishes a precedent that may help retain top talent, provides continuity, and substantially shortens the new executive's learning curve.

A board considering this, however, should first consult extensively with faculty and other constituents to gauge support for the candidate and conduct no less due diligence than if it were doing a full search.

---

[7] *American College President 2012*, p. 41.

---

interview someone they have never met. But handling an internal candidate differently from others being considered can have unfortunate consequences.

It is unethical, unfair and a waste of time to conduct a search where an inside candidate is the presumptive choice in the eyes of the search committee and board. If an inside candidacy is so strong that this is the case, the board should instead do its full due diligence and, if everything checks out, enter into negotiations that can lead to direct appointment *(see sidebar)*.

Key Points

- **Departing presidents may be asked to stay engaged during the search** or (if the new president agrees) beyond. But the relationship should be carefully crafted and well understood.

- **An acting or interim president can help stabilize a campus in turmoil**, address short-term challenges, maintain institutional momentum, or set the stage for a successful search.

- **Consider carefully the pros and cons of having internal candidates.** If any do apply for the opening, they should be treated as much as possible like other candidates.

- **In some cases, direct appointment of an inside candidate may be warranted.**

Additional Article from *Trusteeship*

Guardo, Carol J. "An Interim President Sets the Stage." *Trusteeship* (March/April 2006): p. 29.

For more recommended reading, see Resources at the end of this book.

Part

II | FRAMEWORK FOR THE FUTURE: PLANNING THE SEARCH

4. Selecting a Search Firm or Consultant

5. The Search Committee

6. Organizing the Search

7. Defining the Institution's Leadership Needs

Chapter 4

Selecting a Search Firm or Consultant

“The process of selecting a search firm is a search in and of itself.”

ARLY IN THE PRESIDENTIAL SEARCH process, most boards decide to employ outside professional help in the form of a search consulting firm. The number of these firms has grown steadily in recent decades, and the large majority of searches—61 percent in 2011—now use them. Among public and independent bachelors, masters, and doctoral institutions, the percentage using consultants is more widespread still, ranging from 68 percent to 81 percent. The exceptions are public bachelors institutions, at 55 percent.[8]

An effective search firm can add substantial value to the process. The consultants bring an industry-wide perspective, developed over time through their work with many individual colleges and universities. This experience enables them to guide client institutions as they grapple with the risks and opportunities of this critical time of transition. Broadly, a search firm can provide the following services:

- Facilitate a board review of institutional strengths and challenges;
- Help guide the identification of a search committee when one has not yet been appointed;

---

[8] Ibid., p. 46.

- Organize the search process and the search committee's work;
- Help develop a position profile;
- Assist in creating a communications plan;
- Manage nominations and applications;
- Provide counsel to applicants;
- Interview references and perform due-diligence checks;
- Organize candidate interviews;
- Advise the search committee on developing its final recommendation to the board; and
- Guide the board and the institution in the transition to a new president.

When selecting a search firm, a transition plan or transition planning group may provide strong guidance. Or the board may delegate the decision to a search committee, once the latter is constituted. But the board, or at least its executive committee or transition planning group, should ultimately approve the choice. The process of selecting a search firm is a search in and of itself. Taking the time to find the right firm will repay the effort.

ADVANTAGES OF USING A SEARCH FIRM

A search firm's principal value springs from three characteristics:

- *Objectivity:* From their neutral vantage point, search consultants are well positioned to help the search committee see the college or university as others see it and then fashion appropriate, responsive search strategies. They can represent an institution in balanced, honest terms that may appeal to candidates leery of a sales job or an uncritical depiction by an insider. Because they are sensitive to candidates' needs and concerns, candidates may find it easier to pose hard questions to them and be more inclined to trust the answers.

- *Connections:* Consultants use their professional networks to spread the word of an opening and then identify and vet candidates. They understand that many of the best prospects are unlikely to apply because they are happily serving in other positions. Consultants can pique the interest of these candidates who might in some successful searches constitute a good half of the semifinalists. As honest brokers, they can persuade them to explore the opportunity and assure them of the confidentiality that a professionally directed search will provide.

- *Proficiency:* Consultants know from experience how searches can be organized and carried out, and they can advise when hard choices must be made or crises emerge. Because they understand the importance of consensus building, they will involve constituencies in a careful examination of the institution's current and future needs. Consultants also have extensive experience in developing and screening a pool of diverse candidates, conducting interviews, interviewing references, and performing background checks. They can also give important assurance to external candidates if the pool includes internal ones.

A search firm's services also include time-consuming work that otherwise would need to be delegated to the search committee or support staff on top of normal workloads and search-related responsibilities. Although working with a search consultant is not inexpensive, the cost is typically much less than that of a failed search, which in most cases would require a new one. And it is far less than the cost of selecting someone who is not up to the job.

Concerns about financial impact often lead boards to debate whether to engage a search consultant. After interviewing a handful of firms, they tend to realize that a consultant's guidance and extensive higher education network will significantly enhance the search. Their members feel more secure knowing that a consultant provides an outside perspective and helps to establish an inclusive process. In many ways, boards often conclude, the careful selection of a search firm can be an insurance policy against unsatisfactory outcomes. It is perhaps the most important step the board can take to improve the odds of a successful search.

CONCERNS ABOUT USING A SEARCH FIRM

As the board begins to explore the option of engaging a search firm, some questions and concerns may arise:

- *Cost:* Search firms often charge one-third of the first year's salary and benefits of the person selected or a minimum flat fee, whichever is higher. Some only

> **"In many ways, boards often conclude, the careful selection of a search firm can be an insurance policy against unsatisfactory outcomes."**

charge a flat fee. Additional costs include general overhead and direct expenses (for travel, advertising, and other related costs). Some boards lack the resources to absorb those costs easily, and some calculate that they can do the job for less by relying on those within the institution.

• *Internal experience:* Some colleges and universities feel that the search process does not require specialized expertise. Many draw candidates from a group of peer institutions, and most of these individuals will become aware of the opening as a matter of course. Winnowing the prospect pool and interviewing are familiar tasks for many in higher education. Many state systems provide central-office guidance to searches at member campuses.

• *Dedication to the institution's needs:* Even though most search consultants have long experience in higher education—often as faculty, deans, or presidents—some boards will doubt that they can understand and value properly what makes a particular campus distinctive. A more serious reservation is that they might not have the institution's best interests at heart. Will they start afresh, or will they hope to place candidates left over from previous searches? Will they push candidates at more than one client institution simultaneously? Will they be scouting talent on our campus for their use in future searches?

• *Client control:* Some boards may be concerned that a consultant could take a directive rather than a consensual approach to the search. Boards and search committees can become too deferential to a consultant's expertise, ceding their direction. Internal control is critical to any presidential search, and a high-handed consultant who does not hear and adjust to a client's concerns is clearly problematic.

SELECTING A SEARCH FIRM

Despite such concerns, most boards decide that securing a consultant's services is preferable to going it alone. The vetting of search firms typically is done by the board's executive committee, an ad hoc or standing transition planning group, or a search committee (once it is constituted). The recommendation then comes to the full board for adoption. Moving through the following steps, the group charged with the selection gets increasing clarity on what different firms offer and then selects a few to interview in person.

- *Identify prospects:* For basic information on the universe of search consultants with experience in higher education, review search firms' websites and printed literature; online announcements of current presidential searches at colleges and universities that are similar to yours in size, mission, and the like; and announcements in publications like the *Chronicle of Higher Education*. Contact board or search committee chairs at peer institutions that have recently worked with search firms to hone in on a few candidates. Ask about the consultants' strengths, weaknesses, and the institutions' general level of satisfaction with their work.

- *Invite proposals:* Set up phone interviews with a small group of consultants, and then invite those that seem to best fit your needs to submit brief written proposals that address their values and general approach, distinctiveness, relevant experience, capacity and staffing, and initial thoughts about your institution's competitive position and prospects. In addition, ask them to list the major elements of a proposed search, typical contract terms, and the like.

FINDING THE RIGHT SEARCH FIRM

- **Read** prospective search firms' literature and websites carefully;
- **Compare** the firms' experience with the needs of the institution;
- **Research individual consultants' experience** at similar institutions;
- **Conduct phone interviews** with, and request proposals from, three to five firms;

- **Inquire** about the experience, staffing, search model, suggested timeline, and final selection process;
- **Obtain an estimate** of the full cost, including fees and expenses, in writing; and
- **Conduct in-person interviews** with, and check the references of, a narrowed short list of two or three firms.

- *Invite presentations:* Choose a handful of firms to make hour-long presentations, including a question-and-answer session, ideally within one day. It is reasonable to expect that the consultant who would be conducting your search would represent the firm on this occasion. When one or two firms have risen to the top, check their references carefully and seek out references from others who have worked with them. Any firm eliminated from consideration will appreciate being notified promptly. A second or final interview with the whole group may be in order, especially if not all members of the search committee (or other group) have been able to attend the prior presentation.

DEVELOPING A CONTRACT

Before the board is asked to approve a choice, the preferred search consultant should provide still more detail in the form of a full proposal and contract, based on the following questions:

- What services does the search consultant provide? *(See "Summary of the Roles in a Presidential Search," page 39.)*
- How does the consultant typically work with a search committee and board?
- What proportion of the pool would he or she expect to generate?
- What is the projected timeline?
- For budgeting purposes, what is the search likely to cost, once all expenses (consultant's fees, institutional overhead, search committee travel, candidates' travel, entertainment, relocation expenses, and so on) are included?
- How will the firm's services be billed?
- How will the institution be protected against untoward consequences? Will the firm guarantee, for example, to conduct another search at no cost should the individual chosen leave the position within some period (often a year) because he or she is an inappropriate fit? Will the firm agree that the new president, and possibly all those reporting directly to him or her, will be off-limits to other searches the firm might conduct in a given period?

SUMMARY OF THE ROLES IN A PRESIDENTIAL SEARCH

Responsibiliities	Board	Search Committee	Search Consultant*	Institutional Staff
Decide whether or not to hire a search firm	✓			
Vet search firms (if applicable)	✓	✓		
Allot funds for the search	✓			
Establish timeline	✓	✓	✓	
Communicate with campus community		✓		
Advertise the search and recruit candidates		✓	✓	
Consult with internal stakeholders	✓	✓	✓	
Develop position profile		✓	✓	
Coordinate scheduling and logistics		✓	✓	✓
Evaluate applicants		✓	✓	
Perform due-diligence checks		✓	✓	
Select finalists for interviews		✓		
Make the offer	✓			
Develop transition plan	✓		✓	✓

* If a search firm is retained, the consultant may perform some or all of the checked duties in place of or in collaboration with the search committee.

Adapted from *Presidential Search: An Overview for Board Members* (AGB Press, 2012)

Carefully anticipating and addressing all these questions while a search awaits—or looms as an urgent priority—can take some time and patience. But identifying the right consultant and developing a shared understanding as to expectations, goals, and work to be done is critical and worth the investment.

Key Points

- **A capable search consultant provides an objective view** of the institution, a large network of prospects and contacts, tested skill with the process and logistics of a search, and experience in matching candidates with institutions.

- **Evaluate search firms carefully to find the best fit** with the institution and its needs. A good selection greatly improves the odds of a successful effort.

- **Develop a sound contract that includes a budget, a timeline, and expectations** as to deliverables and division of labor.

Chapter 5

The Search Committee

> **66 Search committees come in different sizes. 99**

FACED WITH THE NEED to secure a new president, virtually all college and university governing boards create a search committee to develop a pool of candidates, screen them, and recommend finalists. Working in close coordination, the committee and the search firm contracted with by the board represent the interests of the board and the campus community to the candidates. They exercise discretion and professionalism in their work on recruitment, applicant communications, and assessment of candidate fit. They bear the weight of the entire community's expectations. The board in particular extends them its trust.

Ideally, transition planning has prepared the way for this delegation of responsibility with specific guidance as described in Chapter 1. If a prior plan exists, the board will want to review it carefully for currency and make any necessary adjustments. Absent a succession plan, the committee's composition and charge will need to be decided among the board's first orders of business. The search committee typically includes a number of board members and members of other key constituencies as well. How the latter are chosen deserves careful thought. So does the charge, detailing the committee's resources and responsibilities, including regular communication and updates. Having selected the group and charged it, the board should then leave the committee to do its job, which is ultimately to recommend final candidates to the board. No search committee should do more. The board alone will select and appoint a new president.

FORMING THE SEARCH COMMITTEE

Search committees come in different sizes. Memberships sometimes reach or exceed 20, but the consensus among those who work extensively with search committees seems to be that an ideal size is in the range of seven to 12, which should allow for appropriately broad representation. A larger group (increasingly seen in recent years in public searches) can be unwieldy and have limited ability to work as a team with strong shared interests in confidentiality and the common good. But most would endorse adding a few members beyond 12 if they include, say, a key constituency or two and help secure the confidence of the community.

Because governing boards are ultimately responsible for leadership transitions, boards alone (frequently their executive committees) appoint search committees. Usually, more than half of the members are board members. They should come from among established and emerging board leadership, and they should be individuals who plan to remain on the board at least for a year or two into the new presidency.

The search committee chair should be a board member, and is in fact often the board's vice chair. He or she is usually designated by the full board but sometimes elected by the search committee. The chair embodies the board's authority and bears responsibility for carrying out the committee's charge. He or she should command the respect of committee members and the campus community, set the tone for the committee's work, and model the behaviors expected of all members. The chair needs leadership qualities that include:

- Impartiality, diplomacy, tact, a sense of humor, and common sense;
- The ability to inspire and persuade;
- Deep knowledge of the institution and a grasp of its politics;
- The capacity to see the big picture;
- Skill at process management; and
- A sense of when to let a discussion run and when to press for a conclusion.

The chair must also be able to listen to candidates' concerns and convey the excitement of the opportunity in a compelling manner. Throughout the search, his or her actions will shape public perception of the integrity of the process and of the institution itself.

> ❝ **The board chair in most cases should not chair the search committee.** ❞

The board chair in most cases should not chair the search committee. One concern is often the matter of availability; many board chairs have crushing schedules that would make it difficult to take this on. Another concern is fit for the job. Board chairs may bring almost too much authority to the role, and their opinions may receive more deference than is useful. Especially if the board chair is a strong personality, who might tend to dominate the committee or push for a favorite candidate over general opposition, there is a case for other leadership. The board chair might also consider that his or her principal function is to guide the final selection, a function that could be compromised through participation in the screening process. Observer status for the board chair during interviews and screenings is always a possibility, provided everyone understands that deliberations should not be reported to non-committee board members.

The search committee chair and the board chair should candidly discuss and agree on their respective roles. A critical point to clarify is the choice of one to be the spokesperson and contact for inquiries about the search process. In any event, the search committee chair should communicate regularly, fully, and in confidence with the board chair about the committee's progress and key issues it might be facing.

In most cases, the participation of non-board members on a search committee is by invitation. Absent bylaws or state regulations dictating their membership by virtue of their position, participation is a privilege, not a legal right. Boards should recognize, however, that their goal is to give the incoming president maximum credibility and acceptance among key constituent groups, and that argues for the appropriate inclusion of representatives of these groups in the search process. What does that inclusion look like and how is it best secured? Answers vary widely from search to search according to the size, complexity, politics, traditions, and culture of the institution.

Most boards recognize first the legitimate concern of the faculty in the selection process. In public institutions, state statutes often require faculty to be part of the process. As stewards and agents of the academic and research missions of the institution, and often with decades-long commitments of service, faculty members have a strong claim to representation. "Joint effort" is specifically recommended in the formal Statement on Government of Colleges and Universities, issued in 1966 by the American Association of University Professors and commended by AGB as a significant step toward clarifying the respective roles of governing boards, faculties, and administrators.[9] Selected alumni, students, administrators (sometimes excepting those likely to be direct reports), staff, and members of the broader community are commonly appointed as additional members. In public higher education, the, chief executives and board members of university foundations typically have a representative on the search committee as well.

An issue to think about carefully is just how these non-board members are chosen and nominated, all subject to board approval. Search committees generally take one of three approaches:

1. ***Board selection:*** The board identifies one or more representatives from each of several stakeholder groups (for example, faculty, alumni association, and student government association) and appoints them. This approach denies anyone but the board a voice in the process.

2. ***Constituent group selection:*** The board asks each constituent group to select a representative to the search committee, in keeping with specific criteria that the committee develops. This approach can sometimes yield individuals who are not suitable for the role.

3. ***Constituent group recommendation and board selection:*** The board asks each constituent group to recommend several possibilities, and the board selects from among them.

Whatever the approach to search committee composition, it should help the board launch and manage a functioning, productive process while demonstrating appropriate concern for the diversity of legitimate interests affected by the search. Inclusion need

---

[9] The statement reads in part: "The selection of a chief administrative officer should follow upon cooperative search by the governing board and the faculty, taking into consideration the opinions of others who are appropriately interested."

not mean, however, that every group is represented. At the same time, some individuals may be chosen in part because they could represent several. One advantage of a single appointing authority is that it can ensure that another important goal is met: some overall diversity and balance in gender, race, ethnicity, and other relevant factors.

Collectively, committee members should bring an array of skills and frames of reference to their assignment. With members, as with the chair, personal and professional qualities are important. They include:

- Stature, expertise, and ability that are readily apparent to the community;
- Knowledge of the institution and its aspirations and willingness to learn still more;
- Ability to rise above parochial concerns and mesh with a group that commits to serving the interests of the institution as a whole; and
- Ability and willingness to maintain the search's confidentiality, even after it concludes.

THE SEARCH COMMITTEE'S CHARGE

At many state-controlled institutions, state authorities spell out search committee goals and processes in advance, often with particular attention to budget and legal issues. In other settings, as a board moves to establish a search committee, it should draft a clear written statement of the committee's mandate. If the board elects to leave procedural details largely to the committee without a clear general charge, the committee is likely to run into difficulty. The extent and limits of its responsibilities may come into question—either among the members themselves or among others outside their circle.

A clear charge might include the following tasks, most of which are addressed elsewhere in this book:

- Selecting a search firm *(Chapter 4)*;
- Developing policies and procedures for the search *(Chapter 6)*;
- Conducting an analysis of the institution's future needs and opportunities and formulating a position statement based on the analysis *(Chapter 7)*;
- Generating a strong and diverse pool of candidates through advertisements and direct recruitment *(Chapter 8)*;

- Managing the applicant pool and keeping all candidates aware of their status *(Chapter 8)*;
- Screening the candidate pool *(Chapter 9)*;
- Interviewing selected candidates *(Chapter 9)*;
- Performing due diligence, including reference and background checks *(Chapter 9)*;
- Identifying finalists *(Chapter 10)*;
- Planning and conducting campus visits *(Chapter 12)*;
- Providing recommendations to the board *(Chapter 12)*;
- Keeping the board apprised appropriately throughout the process; and
- In strict accordance with a search communications plan, keeping the community apprised appropriately as well.

The charge to the search committee should ensure that the board's responsibility to select and appoint a president is in no way compromised or preempted, a concern that bears on the form and number of the search committee's recommendations. Does the board, for example, want the search committee to forward a single recommendation? This course might be the most efficient but, in effect, it delegates the board's responsibility for selection. Serious problems could arise if the board does not support the choice or if that individual declines the board's offer. Even a ranked set of several recommended candidates may be regarded as tying the board's hands by putting it in a position of needing to overturn a recommendation should its independent review order the candidates differently. In contrast, an unranked selection of three to five highly qualified, thoroughly vetted candidates gives the board options, flexibility, and a good chance of a successful appointment.

Charges to search committees are sometimes relatively extensive, sometimes short and simple *(see Appendix A)*. They may include the following points:

- Require that the search committee's work be in keeping with all applicable laws, policies, and the like;
- Describe the scope of the search, which can be national or even global;
- Express the expectation that the committee will make a special effort to generate a diverse applicant pool;

- Outline a timetable, or at least the date by which a new presidency should begin;
- Provide a preliminary budget;
- State a range of compensation that can be shared selectively with serious candidates;
- Describe the expected degree of openness with the board; and
- Express the importance of confidentiality. (Some boards ask search committee members to sign a code of ethics statement addressing this point, conflicts of interest, and other such concerns.)

The full board should approve the charge and present it formally to the search committee. It is sometimes posted publicly (in printed notices and online)—with any code of ethics—as witness to the great importance of this board responsibility.

Key Points

- **The search committee is the institution's public face** during the process of finding a new president.

- **Form a search committee that is broadly representative of the institution's constituencies.** Its members should be well respected for their competence and knowledge of the institution and able to rise above parochial interests.

- **The board member who chairs the committee must be an effective leader**: impartial, inspirational, knowledgeable, and skilled at directing group deliberations.

- **Detail the search committee's responsibilities in a formal written charge from the board.** The committee's work must not preempt the board's duty to select and appoint a president.

Chapter 6

Organizing the Search

> **"Search committees... tend to start slowly and end in a rush."**

BEFORE THE SEARCH COMMITTEE'S WORK can get underway, the responsible people or groups—which may include board leadership, the transition committee, the search committee chair, the search committee, and the search consultant—will need to make a series of decisions regarding approaches, policies, and procedures. They will want to work within parameters already set, but they are likely also to need to tackle key topics on which there has been no guidance. Their decisions will go far toward organizing the committee for the tasks ahead.

Careful planning and organization will ensure that no important step will be overlooked. Not coincidentally, planning informs members unfamiliar with academic searches (possibly the majority of the committee) what to expect. It also spares the committee chair the need to make ad hoc decisions at every turn. To prepare itself for an efficient and effective search, the committee should:

- Set an orderly schedule that committee members can place on their calendars;
- Identify the available resources, including budget, staffing, and workspace needs;

- Agree on internal norms and procedures, including how the committee will communicate its work to others;
- Establish the openness of the search and ensure its compliance with applicable laws, regulations, and policies; and
- Provide for thorough recordkeeping throughout the process.

TIMETABLE

Search committees, like legislatures, tend to start slowly and end in a rush. It is not just that the final deadline seems at first a comfortable distance away; committees frequently underestimate the time required and the cumulative impact of inevitable delays. A realistic timetable should be set at the start of operations. *(For an example, see Appendix B.)* Experienced search consultants can recommend ways to greatly increase efficiency, saving committee members time while still allowing full, responsible involvement in the process.

At a minimum, the search committee should expect in its charge a firm date by which a new president is to assume office. Working backward from that date, the board leadership, transition committee, search committee chair, and/or consultant can determine the search schedule. When a resigning president gives ample notice, he or she often times the departure to suit the requirements of the search effort and a direct and graceful handoff to a successor. By contrast, a hurried departure (or a wish not to have an incumbent continue in office any longer than necessary) can clearly require the appointment of an interim president. If the board finds itself in a grey area, unsure whether it has the time to complete a search for a permanent successor by a desired start date, it may want to consider two questions: *What is the likely length of the search?* and *What is the preferred season for conducting the search?*

Searches ordinarily take about four to six months from beginning to end, excluding summers (the summer months may be better for preparing than for searching). The length varies depending on factors such as:

- The sense of urgency behind the effort;
- The time within the academic calendar that the search takes place; and

- The search's overall efficiency and its success in hitting key targets (for example, gathering selected candidates for on-campus interviews at the time originally planned).

When setting the schedule, consider the time needed for the newly selected leader to announce his or her departure from a current position and transition from it responsibly. Anticipate, as well, the possible need for additional time should the committee or board fail to agree on a candidate or the individual selected decline the offer. The vicissitudes of travel, weather, and other uncertainties will call for some flexibility. The board usually will want to schedule a special meeting to take action on the committee's recommendations. The decision is too important to be an agenda item at a regular board meeting.

Once a timetable is approved, it should be presented to the search committee, with recommended times for the five to seven in-person meetings the committee typically requires. Getting dates and times (beginning and ending) for all meetings on all members' calendars from the outset is an important step. The goal—which some searches actually meet—is to have every member present for every significant committee decision.

BUDGET

Searches tend to be far more expensive than most boards imagine. It is important to know in advance what costs to expect and be able to budget effectively to meet them—and to plan the search committee's work with an eye to what the institution can and cannot afford.

As mentioned in Chapter 4, search firms typically charge a fee that is a third of the new president's first year's compensation (defined variously by different firms) or a flat fee, whichever is higher. Sometimes the firm charges only a flat fee, and the fee may sometimes be negotiable. It may or may not cover the firm's expenses for items such as photocopying, conference calls, overnight delivery, and other variable charges incurred in connection with the search. Travel and travel-related costs will be billed separately, as will the cost of advertising the position. If consultants are not used, the work they would do will need to be done locally, and comparable direct expense—except for the consultant's travel—and overhead will need to be absorbed. At least for estimating full costs, the salary and other expenses of this work should be charged to the effort.

The full cost of a search, however, also includes: administrative and clerical support at the institution, needed even when a consultant is retained; travel, lodging, and meals for committee members and candidates; the cost of background checks on final candidates; and any consultation required by specialists on contracts, compensation, and the like. Relocation expenses may figure in, as well.

The cost of most searches is in the low six figures. *(For a sample budget, see Appendix C.)* With good planning, costs projected at a daunting level can be made somewhat more manageable. But the selection of the new president is so vital to the life of the institution—and the selection of the wrong one potentially so disastrous—that this is no place to risk failure through false economy. The successful candidate will be managing an enterprise with a budget in the tens or hundreds of millions. Given the unhappy alternative, the cost of finding the right person is clearly a worthwhile investment.

STAFF AND RECORDKEEPING

Selecting a president involves a considerable amount of logistical detail, from scheduling committee meetings, to establishing a secure information management system, to arranging interviews. A search firm will often take responsibility for many of these tasks. But even so, the institution will need responsible staff assistance, and the firm's and staff member's respective responsibilities will need to be clearly identified and closely coordinated. If a consultant is not retained, the committee will still need to see that all this work is done. In most situations, this means assigning at least one staff member to the search. This person should know the institution, have the respect of its various constituencies, and be discreet and capable. Though the staff member may not need to give full time to the assignment, he or she must be able to put the search first during crunch times. Over a six-month search, these responsibilities might consume about one-third of his or her time.

Institutions that have designated board professionals will probably want to entrust them with this part of the process. Varying amounts of administrative and clerical help may be needed as the search effort moves forward. The staff assistant must be prepared to work closely with the search committee chair, its members, and the consultant if one has been retained. And of course, he or she must comply fully with the committee's policies on confidentiality and disclosure.

A complete, organized, and easily retrievable record of official actions is important for keeping the search process on track. Consideration of many candidates over many weeks and months breeds confusion. Memories become dim or erratic. The records may need to be consulted frequently even as the search unfolds. The advice of legal counsel will be important in setting up a recordkeeping system. Its contents may be subject to the open-records laws mentioned later in this chapter. If they are, demands made under the law tend to be non-negotiable and can be made on short notice.[10] Careful documentation also records the committee's compliance with regulations regarding equal opportunity and affirmative action in building the candidate pool. *(See Chapter 9.)*

A key resource for the committee will be a public website devoted to the search, easily accessible to all by a link from the institutional site's home page. This site will be a primary means for communication with the campus as well as external constituencies, including potential candidates prior to the point of application. The search committee will also need its own site for the confidential conduct of its work. As a part of the administrative support that a search firm typically provides, it will create and maintain a section on its own website for the client institution's search. Candidates' electronic files will be posted there and made accessible to search committee members and search firm staff only. Committee members have the online address and a password, so they can then review files at any time.

COMMITTEE NORMS AND PROCEDURES

How the search committee's members wish to work together is a matter best left to them to decide. And the fewer rules the better. But some understandings are clearly desirable. Teams work best in an environment of candor, mutual respect, and informality. Members who can agree to extend the courtesies of regular attendance and punctuality, do their homework on time, and fully participate and contribute to consensus make each other's work easier and more enjoyable—and the committee's work more effective. Those who are confident that their views are heard and respected, and who feel they can dissent without being regarded as obstructionist, will be able to focus on the task without dis-

---

[10] Rachel Levinson-Waldman and Robert M. O'Neil, "Growing Demands for Public Records: Should Boards Respond?" *Trusteeship*, January/February 2012, p. 23.

traction. Individual complaints about the process or decisions made should be brought promptly to the chair's attention (and no one should grumble privately or to outsiders). Guidelines that promote these conditions should be established early.

A rule-bound way of conducting business—through motions and formal votes—is unlikely to serve the group well. Consensus, however hard-won, is the ideal in search committee work. Deciding by consensus does not mean that every person agrees but that each will have his or her say until there is a "sense of the whole." Then the committee moves on. Fortunately, most search committees do gradually develop such a sense not only around specific candidates, but also around their collective identity as a functioning group. Individuals tend increasingly to transcend particular loyalties and to focus on institutional needs. As they do this, consensus becomes increasingly more possible.

Clearly, conflicts of interest—real or perceived—can undermine a committee's cohesiveness and effectiveness, not to mention its external credibility. A search committee member might nominate and advocate a particular candidate and then try to influence other committee members to support this candidate. Or a committee member may be a close professional and personal colleague of a candidate, and, instead of recusing herself when discussing candidate attributes and fit, fully engages in the conversation and consideration. Members should discuss how and where in the process conflicts like these might arise and decide how they will be dealt with when they do.

COMPLIANCE

Early on, the search committee will benefit from briefings from two key resources: the university's legal counsel and its affirmative-action officer. The legal counsel will address federal equal-opportunity legislation, which applies to all programs receiving federal funds, as well as any related state laws. He or she can describe specifically how they apply to the conduct of the search. For publicly supported institutions, the attorney's interpretation of state open-meeting laws will prove invaluable. The affirmative-action officer will be more specifically concerned with board-mandated personnel policies. A search consultant will be generally acquainted with these policies, as well. He or she can distill from the accumulated experience of many searches specific guidance about reviewing credentials, interviewing, and other forms of information gathering.

In colleges or universities that are part of a multi-campus system, the search consultant or committee also will want to consult a system representative about the central office's expectations. Systems that allow constituent campuses to conduct presidential searches—a number do not, reserving that responsibility to system-wide governing boards—vary widely in the degree of influence they exert. Some have detailed codes regulating the conduct of searches, while others

> **" A presidential search offers an unprecedented opportunity to enhance the university's standing among its many constituencies. "**

have only informal expectations. In some states, a designee from the central office serves on each presidential search; in others, expert advice is provided through a professional consultant hired to help the committee formulate its search plan or to review the plan after it has been drafted. In some systems, a uniform presidential job description applies to all campuses, while in others the board has the opportunity to compose a unique description. Occasionally, system personnel policies apparently unrelated to the presidency may impinge upon the selection—for example, policies related to the award of tenure.

CONFIDENTIALITY AND COMMUNICATION

A presidential search offers an unprecedented opportunity to enhance the university's standing among its many constituencies. Interest in the search, although especially intense on campus, will extend well beyond its boundaries, beyond alumni, even beyond the local community. Because a president embodies the aspirations of a university and its vision of the future, peer institutions, professional associations, funding organizations and other benefactors, perhaps state legislatures, and most assuredly the media will monitor the selection closely. Nominations may come from many of these groups, and many more will read stories about the search. Before the final choice is announced, many people will be touched in one way or another by the search committee's actions.

Before the search begins, the committee should formulate its policy in two areas: 1) confidentiality, including what information will be disclosed, when, and to whom; and 2) external communication, including who is authorized to speak for the committee and what form that communication will take. This policy involves, at a minimum, keeping all interested parties fully and accurately informed. But releasing *too much* information can embarrass candidates and may result in losing them—or in failing to attract them to begin with. Releasing *too little* information can offend constituents and may invite distrust and rumors.

In public institutions, state open-meeting and open-record laws may impose specific requirements on the search process, dictating policy about confidentiality and communication. There is great variation, however, in the stringency of such laws. Many states exempt personnel matters from public scrutiny, thus allowing search committees a significant measure of privacy, at least while the search is taking place. Other states have freedom of information laws requiring all state business to be conducted "in the sunshine"—that is, in public view.

Confidentiality

Most who conduct searches—and most candidates—would prefer that the process be kept confidential. Complete public disclosure may reduce the number of top candidates because the best-qualified individuals often need to be recruited and cultivated in confidence. Candidates know that publicity can jeopardize their position or standing in their present institutions, and public discussion of their merits may well be embarrassing to them if they are not selected. Most will at least insist on knowing they are finalists before allowing their names to be released.

The campus community, the public, and the media, on the other hand, want to know what is going on. While the identity of candidates is something to hold close as long as possible, the composition of the committee, its mandate, the procedures it proposes to follow, and its progress are legitimate matters of public interest and should be explained carefully to students, faculty, alumni, and the public. It is helpful to disclose these details when the search is announced—for example, why candidates' names are confidential until a certain time, when they will be announced, and what the overall timeline will be.

Candidates will want to know at the outset whether confidentiality will be maintained. More is at stake than courtesy (although courtesy should not be ignored). On-campus and inter-campus grapevines are robust and far-reaching, and more than one career has suffered because a search committee member has mentioned a name. Early in one search process, the name of a prominent sitting president was publicly disclosed. The candidate's home campus was in the midst of a capital campaign, and some reliable donors and board members were so concerned that the president might leave for another institution that they became hesitant to contribute. Such occurrences are less likely if a search committee is apprised of the possible consequences of revealing a candidate's identity. No one wants to be responsible for disrupting a career or frightening off promising candidates.

Of course, the identities of the finalists will almost always be disclosed because most searches require that they make a public visit to the campus. These visits are an important opportunity for faculty, administration, and local constituencies to see and size up the candidates, and they give candidates a chance to appraise the institution. Finalists should be aware of this expectation early in the search process. In fact, candidates should be advised in advance if at any time it is necessary to make public their identities and biographies. They may prefer to withdraw, and they should, in fairness, be given an opportunity to do so.

Breaches of promised confidentiality and refusals to provide information will inevitably cause problems. The most common breach occurs by leaks, endemic in modern life and particularly in politicized situations. Search committees need to be especially vigilant, for example, when the departure of the last president has left a troubled campus, when one or more internal candidates have local supporters or critics, or when persistent reporters are seeking stories.

To help prevent leaks, some search committees ask each member to sign a letter of confidence or a code of ethics that addresses confidentiality, among other matters. The committee may indicate that if the member violates confidence, he or she will be removed. To provide further disincentive, some agreements even state that the reasons for the removal will be made public.

Communication Outside the Committee

If the search is not subject to restrictive sunshine laws and if the committee has agreed to the principle of confidentiality, then it must decide what information to disclose, when, to whom, and by whom.

Who speaks for the committee? This question is straightforward. If several people respond to inquiries, particularly those relating to policy, confusion will ensue. The spokesperson ordinarily will be the search committee's chair; in some cases, it might be the board chair. In either case, this individual should be assisted by the institution's senior public relations officer. All inquiries should be referred to the spokesperson, all correspondence will bear his or her signature, and he or she will speak for the committee on all public occasions. The aim is to ensure consistent, politic messages and to shield committee members from questions from colleagues and the media.

What information to disclose, when, to whom? By demeanor and language, the committee's spokesperson will shape public perceptions of the search and of the university itself. In satisfying the intense curiosity surrounding a presidential search and promoting a sense of inclusion on campus, a policy of forthrightness is advantageous. All constituencies should be kept informed of the progress of the search, and the information provided should be as complete as possible, consistent with the requirements of confidentiality. Although names and titles will not be disclosed (unless required by law), statistical data (number of applicants and geographic distribution) should pose no problem.

Decision points for communication. A series of decision points punctuates every search, marking the completion of one phase and the start of the next. These points are natural occasions for web postings, faculty bulletins, alumni news reports, and media releases summarizing progress:

- Announcement of the search;
- Appointment of the search committee;
- Completion of the position announcement, including the qualities sought in a new president, and announcement of a recruiting program;
- Announcement of finalists; and
- Selection and appointment of the new president.

Communications at most of these points cannot discuss candidates but should be as complete as possible on procedures and progress. Appearing at regular intervals, bulletins appease the hunger for information and slow the rumor mill. More important, they build a sense of momentum and expectation that ultimately translates into an enthusiastic welcome for the new president.

Two constituencies beyond the campus community have particular needs to be kept informed of the status of the search:

- **Candidates:** The pool of applicants must be kept informed of the status of their candidacies, the progress of the search, and the date when the next committee action will occur. As screening narrows the field, those no longer under consideration need to be promptly informed. Those retained should receive more complete information about the institution, both to keep their interest alive and to enlarge their understanding of what the presidency requires. *(Appendix E outlines materials to provide in each stage of the search process.)*

- **Media:** Dealings with the print and electronic media, on campus and off, should be strategically planned and managed. Given the symbiotic way in which the media can work with their subjects—the latter providing copy, the former visibility—they are potentially very useful vehicles for getting widespread attention to key institutional messages.

To both the campus community and the press, the committee will want to communicate positive messages: The search is in good hands. The institution's mission and needs are foremost concerns. Its future is bright. The community is engaged. Many people deserve thanks. Appropriate materials should be prepared for each audience, and press access to the committee spokesperson should be provided. Their requests for information should be answered, if possible, with two notable exceptions: the identity of prefinalist candidates and the content of the committee's deliberations. Some members of the media may be aggressive in their pursuit, but a forthcoming attitude can help to create a productive and mutually cooperative relationship.

When possible, those seeking information should be directed to the public website devoted to the search. The search announcement and application details, the search committee membership and charge, the search consultant's contact information, and a timetable can all be posted there. In a public institution where open searches are mandated, still more information may be considered or even required.

Special Issues for Public Institutions

Mandated openness in presidential searches creates an inherent tension among the public's right to know, the individual's right to privacy, and the institution's ability to conduct the kind of search that will secure the leadership it needs to serve its largely public purposes.[11] When sunshine laws apply to a search, what suffers is the search committee's ability to obtain and deliberate on highly sensitive information about candidate backgrounds and prior performance. According to Vanderbilt University professors James Hearn and Michael McClendon, who have studied this area, higher education leaders agree that public input is important, but many are concerned that "conducting searches entirely in the open may have a 'chilling effect' that dilutes both the quality and the quantity of applicants."[12] Candidates—particularly sitting presidents—may fear what might happen should their interest in a new position come to light. They hear about presidents in the same situation who lose credibility, financial support, or even their jobs. They may also fear embarrassment and reputational damage if they are not chosen.

In some settings, "openness" has been taken to extremes—with, for example, an obligation to disclose publicly every name mentioned to a search committee or consultant (with or without the person's knowledge or consent)[13] or the requirement that a committee's interviews, and even its deliberations, be streamed online.[14] More commonly, when sunshine laws pose real constraints, they require names (and curriculum vitae) to be shared publicly, with permission, before candidates might become finalists.

Search committees affected by open-meeting or open-record requirements sometimes resist the unwanted intrusions, occasionally with extreme measures of their own. They use techniques such as holding meetings out of state, ushering candidates

---

[11] Harlan Cleveland, quoted in James C. Hearn and Michael McLendon, "Choose Public-College Presidents in the Sunshine, but Know When to Draw the Shades," *Chronicle Review*, July 9, 2004.

[12] Ibid.

[13] Dowdall, *Searching for Higher Education Leadership*, p. 93.

[14] Alexandra Tilsley, "Too Much Sunshine Can Complicate Presidential Searches," *Chronicle of Higher Education*, August 8, 2010.

in through back doors to avoid the press, and running a confidential search alongside a public one.

Fortunately, legislatures have seen the need for balance. Many open-meeting laws, for example, allow executive session. Many states have provisions exempting public organizations from the requirement to release the identity of candidates for employment. These changes mean that, for all practical purposes, candidates' names rarely are disclosed.[15]

In public institutions, search committees should maximize the confidentiality of the process to the degree possible within the law, with special emphasis on maintaining the privacy of deliberations and not disclosing the identities of candidates until they are invited and agree to be finalists. In this task, an experienced search consultant may be especially helpful. *(See also "Searches in State University Systems," Chapter 12, page 122.)*

Key Points

- **Ensure compliance** with all applicable laws and regulations— and, in the case of public institutions, with system policies.

- **Commit to a timeline and budget**, secure staff support, and establish a system for keeping records.

- **Encourage consensus decision making** in an atmosphere of candor, mutual respect, and informality to help ensure a productive and rewarding search.

- **Agree on what information will be held in confidence** and what will be communicated publicly, as well as who will speak for the search effort. Decide how openly the search should be conducted.

- **Balance carefully the public's right to know**, the candidate's need for privacy, and the institution's ability to conduct a search. Public institutions must be particularly careful in states that mandate openness in presidential searches.

---

[15] Martin and Samels, *Presidential Transition*, pp. 200–201.

Chapter 7

Defining Leadership Needs

> **"Presidents today face an array of challenges that their predecessors never confronted."**

SUCCESSFUL SEARCHES ARE DRIVEN by careful introspection about institutional needs. This, in turn, supports detailed articulations of the qualities and abilities sought in a new leader and the particular challenges and opportunities he or she should be ready to tackle. Before the process gets under way, the search committee must:

- Assess the status of the institution, and
- Identify key criteria to guide the selection process.

In practice, these two essential tasks are too often ignored. Boards and search committees have a tendency to rush into the search and selection of candidates without collectively taking stock of and agreeing on what or whom the college or university really needs. They often pay the price later, when, far into the process, disparate views of the selection criteria emerge on the committee or in the community or, even worse, when someone is appointed who proves not to have the skills and abilities required for the job. Some decades ago, an American college president was often viewed as a figurehead—albeit an admirable one with seniority and academic distinction. In this stereotypical view, if the president actually did anything other than give speeches and accept checks, he or she oversaw largely self-sustaining institutions. The image was never accurate or fair. But presidents today do face an array of challenges that their predecessors never confronted. In an era of ubiquitous and often disruptive change, their institutions are anything but self-sustaining, requiring extraordinary abilities and efforts of their leaders. Intense global competition, rapid technological developments, economic uncertainty, changing demographics, shifting demands for education and training, new ways of delivering instruction, new pressures for accountability, inadequate public funding—these and other realities create myriad obstacles and opportunities. They challenge and advantage different campuses in different ways, but presidents never have the option of *not* grappling with change. In fact, these realities impose on presidents everywhere the clear obligation to *lead* change. What the board and search committee must decide is exactly what kind of leader their institution requires at this particular time.

PRESIDENTIAL ARCHETYPES

Four archetypes generally emerge from conversations about what higher education institutions need in a president: a manager, an academic leader, a politician, and a fundraiser.

Manager. Many in higher education share a growing conviction that institutions facing existential threats increasingly need presidents with substantial business experience. Whether or not this is always true, these skills clearly will be valued. James Martin and James E. Samels, lead authors of a study that describes the changing profile of presidential leadership, list "new skills" needed and various challenges today's presidents face. Today's leaders are:

- Mastering technology choices related to campus management and student learning;
- Producing partnerships;
- Building a brand;
- Seeking selective excellence;
- Understanding online as well as on-campus education ("clicks" as well as "bricks");
- Leveraging mentoring networks; and

- Ensuring entrepreneurial advantage.[16]

Academic leader. In contrast, some argue that what colleges need more than ever are academic leaders—presidents who understand what makes these institutions distinctive. They prize individuals—often scholars and intellectuals—who can effectively champion the academy's vital role in society as a center of teaching, research, and service.

Politician. A third frequent conception of the president—especially at state-supported institutions—is that of the politician, whose connections and diplomatic and lobbying skills can ensure campus visibility and a fair share of public resources.

Fundraiser. The fourth archetype—the fundraising president—is in fact almost universally embraced in both public and independent institutions.

How these and other concepts of the ideal leader combine in an institution's definition of its needs deserves careful thought and discussion.

Of course, boards should always be as concerned about *who* a president is as they are about what he or she *can do*. Presidencies not only require character and integrity, but they test those traits constantly. Having a good head on one's shoulders and a sense of humor are enormous assets in the job. Any lack of human qualities—for instance, generosity or sensitivity—will soon be detected and undercut a new president's leadership efforts. So will a lack of respect for the need to work with the board. As obvious as these points are, search committees and boards sometimes forget them—to their later regret—when an apparent master of the universe is at hand.

THE PRESEARCH STUDY

To decide exactly what's required, the board should do a presearch study. This institutional needs analysis will inform the development of a position profile. *(See "The Position Profile," later in this chapter.)* Even when the board has ample notice of a president's

---

[16] James Martin and James E. Samels, "A New Model of Transition Management," in Martin and Samels, *Presidential Transition*, pp. 12–18.

departure, there is unlikely to be time for the kind of elaborate self-study it might commission at less critical moments. But it is best practice, before launching a search, for the board and search committee to review the institution's financial health, the relevance and strength of its academic programs, and the adequacy of its personnel. This work needn't take a great deal of time—usually two to three weeks—and it invites the kind of review, debate, and consensus building that will reduce the risk of a premature or misdirected effort. A presearch study substantially increases the odds of a search's success.

A number of existing sources should prove helpful. The strategic plan, if reasonably current, will provide much of what's needed. So will the written products of any recent accreditations or reaccreditations, including both the institution's self-study and the agency's final report. Most colleges and universities have an ongoing institutional research function, which together with the finance office can produce essential data. Also useful are other recent reviews and studies, done on campus or by external consultants. The American Council on Education's periodic study, which creates a comprehensive profile of the American college president, answers questions about who holds these positions, where they come from, and what concerns consume their time and effort.[17]

Inviting Stakeholders to Participate

As part of the presearch study, the search committee should systematically seek the views of the following:

- Board members;
- Search committee members;
- Campus groups, including several representing faculty, staff, students, and alumni; and
- Members of the surrounding community.

Three basic questions provide the framework for stakeholder consultations:

1. What are the attractions of the institution—the strengths and opportunities—that might make it appealing to candidates?
2. What are the needs the institution faces—its weaknesses and challenges?

---

[17] *American College President* (ACE, 2012.)

3. What attributes should we therefore seek in candidates to be our next president?

Board members could respond in writing to the questions and, ideally, discuss them in a board meeting. At a minimum, the board's responses should be shared with the search committee chair. Search committee members should discuss the questions at their first meeting and then brainstorm preferred qualifications. Interviews—based on the three questions—with selected groups on the campus (or with individuals associated with those groups) will also advance the process. The search's public website can also be used effectively to solicit and gather information and ideas.

Holding one or two open meetings is an important way to engage the full campus community in this presearch phase. One large public university, for example, hosted a series of town meetings designed to solicit stakeholder input on topics such as leadership priorities, attributes sought in the new president, and campus needs. A small independent institution asked the search consultant to host small- and large-group meetings to gain input.

Best led by the search committee chair or the search consultant, forums like these can reveal the extent of happiness or discontent on a campus and the degree to which stakeholders agree on key issues. They provide unfiltered views that inform the understanding of the board, the committee, and the consultant and help them

> **66 ...forums can reveal the extent of happiness or discontent on campus. 99**

speak accurately and helpfully with prospective candidates. Candidates know that every campus faces challenges and is enlivened by its own debates and personalities. They appreciate specificity and candor, and for many the challenges will be attractive.[18]

A Dose of Realism

As views and findings emerge, the committee and the search consultant must weigh them judiciously, especially when trying to translate what is learned into a delineation of the attributes sought in a new leader. Some well-known sirens songs are heard along the road to the completed search profile. One—heard most clearly where there is a popular

---

[18] Dowdall, *Searching for Higher Education Leadership,* pp. 95, 97.

incumbent—tempts the community to define the ideal new president as a virtual clone of the current one. Another lures a community weary of a president into describing the ideal successor as his or her polar opposite. A third persuades those doing a search that they can afford to articulate what they want in general terms—a respected academic leader, for example, or someone who can be the face of the college—and then see what they get. Still another invites general and unrealistically lofty expectations. David Warren, president of the National Association of Independent Colleges and Universities, lists among common desiderata, "the fundraising magic of Midas, the vision of Moses, the patience of Job, and the ingenuity of Jonah."[19] These aspirations will ensure disappointing candidates and may suppress interest. And criteria that are too general will not signal to individuals who really do have the right stuff that they will want to look closely at this opening.

THE POSITION PROFILE

After considering the information gathered in the presearch study, the search consultant—in close consultation with the search committee chair—should draft a position profile for discussion and revision at the next search committee meeting and ultimately for approval by the full board.

The position profile serves these purposes:

- Summarizes the mission, history, and accomplishments of the institution;
- Provides an overview of the agenda the institution must address in the next three to five years; and
- Translates institutional challenges into the skills and experiences a president will need to advance that agenda.

The position profile in its most complete form includes information on how to apply, as well as indications of interest in diverse or nontraditional candidates, degrees and experience sought, and the like. It is posted on the search's public website and distributed in print and electronic form. *(For two examples, see Appendix D.)*

---

[19] David Warren, quoted in David L. Marcus, "Why a Good College Chief Is Hard to Find," *U.S. News and World Report*, March 19, 2001.

The presearch survey and subsequent development of the position profile give the community a role in shaping the search and should win the committee additional trust and goodwill. The process also facilitates a growing, if not complete, consensus about key needs. The final profile is the basis for advertisements, requests for nominations, and other forms of recruitment. As a primer on the institution and the position, it will force prospective candidates to write their applications in ways that respond to the relevant criteria.[20] It will also guide the consultant's initial review of applicants as well as the committee's review and recommendations to the board. The search profile is the touchstone against which all candidates can be authoritatively assessed.

This last point is important because search committees—like lonely hearts everywhere—are prone to ill-considered infatuations. Especially as interviews begin, they can find enormously beguiling individuals with winning personalities and other real strengths who nonetheless lack the professional and personal attributes that the presearch study has shown are most necessary. Grounding the profile in real analysis, making the criteria it spells out specific, and *keeping it before everyone* as choices are made are all essential tasks as the search moves ahead.

PRELIMINARY DECISIONS ABOUT COMPENSATION AND ASSESSMENT

As the search committee shapes its list of needs and requirements, it should also anticipate the concerns of candidates. This means deciding at least in general terms what it is prepared to offer. Any good candidate will expect answers to three important questions: How would I be compensated? How would my performance be evaluated? What kind of partnership could I expect to have with the board? It reflects well on the institution to have informed, considered responses ready at the outset of the search, and it could prevent costly missteps.

The committee will want to set at least a salary range and decide other basic elements of the overall compensation package. Transparency in this process is essential, for reasons described later in this book. *(See "Setting Compensation," Chapter 13.)* At

---

[20] Weary in Martin and Samels, "Role of the Board," *Presidential Transition*, p. 70.

this preliminary stage, the board's leadership should do its homework, consulting with the chief financial officer on what the college or university can afford. Basic benchmarks include salaries for senior administrators and senior faculty, along with salaries for comparable positions in the external market. Often search consultants will discuss salary and compensation ranges confidentially with candidates selected for the short list and provide more targeted information before the finalists' campus visits.

A search committee will want to be able to describe to potential candidates a fair and effective system for appraising the new president's performance, so it will look to the board or appropriate board committee for guidance and possibly some improvement to existing assessment practices. If a performance assessment system is not in place—or if the current one could be improved—the outset of the search is the ideal time to attend to this need. To introduce new evaluation arrangements during a term of service naturally raises questions. But to do so between presidencies enables the board and newly appointed leader to begin their work together with shared expectations. The new position profile—endorsed by the board and outlining the new president's tasks—will provide the ideal touchstone. *(See "Providing for Performance Assessment," Chapter 13, for more about evaluation.)*

THE PRESEARCH BOARD SELF-ASSESSMENT

In addition to having concerns about compensation and assessment, candidates understand that no factor is more likely to determine a president's long-term success than his or her working relationship with the board. They also know that even at their best, boards can be demanding. If a prospective applicant or candidate feels that the board would be a supportive and effective partner in overseeing the institution, he or she will view the opportunity more enthusiastically. If not, that fact alone will discourage further interest. The time is ripe, then, before the public launch of a search for the board to look inward and—through surveys, discussions, facilitated retreats, or other means—find ways to improve its own performance. Doing so can significantly strengthen the institution's hand in the competitive arena of presidential search.

The board may need a simple review or a more extensive one, done quickly or requiring ongoing attention through the search period and beyond. The essential outcome is that the board shows candidates its awareness of its responsibilities for the success of both president and institution and its commitment to an ongoing effort to strengthen its own capacity.

Topics for Presearch Self-Assessment

These topics should be included in a presearch board self-assessment or governance audit:

1. ***Board size and composition:*** Is our board so large as to be unwieldy? So small that it is unrepresentative or unable to do all that it should? Is board membership appropriately diverse in terms of race, gender, geography, occupation, skills, and experience? Is membership regularly renewed, and are new members comprehensively oriented? *For public institutions:* Are trustees assertive in advising the appointing authorities of board needs and in supporting an appointment process based on merit?

2. ***Board structure:*** Does our board have the right committees with clear, board-approved charges and adequate leadership? Do committees have the time and resources to do their work? Are committee results reported out effectively to our full board? Can any committees be eliminated because they are moribund or no longer relevant? Is a new committee needed?

3. ***Policies and practices:*** Is there a comprehensive and current policy manual? Are board bylaws—the core legal document defining the board's structure and operation—carefully updated and consistent with applicable laws, board needs, and the highest principles of integrity? Does a statement of board member responsibilities detail expectations for individual members? Is there an adequate code of conduct and ethics and a strong conflict of interest policy?

4. ***Relationship with constituencies:*** Effective communication with faculty, students, and alumni groups is a universal responsibility. How are we doing with each group? Consistent with the dictates of confidentiality, are we informing them of our work? Are we well-informed on their views?

5. ***Relationship with past presidents:*** What has been the history of these rela-

tionships? Was the relationship with the outgoing leader troubled, and, if so, how, if at all, does that reflect on our readiness going forward? The board chair (and his or her likely successors) will be of special interest. Is he or she the kind of working partner most presidents strongly prefer—providing contacts and making introductions, serving as sounding board in a crisis, helping to manage board relations?[21]

6. ***Board dynamics:*** What are the norms of board behavior? Do members attend meetings faithfully? Are they prepared, and do they contribute? Do they "give" or "get"? Are agendas strategic or stale and report-oriented? Is contention allowed to fester? Is real exchange encouraged or is it suppressed by a dominating executive committee? [22]

7. ***Board assessment:*** Do both the full board and individual members take seriously the need to look regularly and honestly at our performance in advancing stated goals? Expecting presidential assessment while exempting the governing board from similar scrutiny can appear hypocritical and can certainly put certain kinds of mutual progress out of reach.

The presearch governance audit discussed here can be an extremely useful precedent for the kind of self-appraisal every board needs to make a regular feature of its work.

Key Points

-   **Taking stock of the institution's strengths**, weaknesses, challenges, and opportunities will help the search committee decide the qualities and abilities most needed in a new president.

-   **The position profile paints a picture of the institution** and its near-term agenda, then describes the skills and experience a new president will need. It becomes a guide for candidates and a touchstone for the search committee.

---

[21] Jean A. Dowdall, "Don't Turn Off Good Candidates," in *Trusteeship*, January/February, 2004, pp. 1–3.

[22] See Weary in Martin and Samels, "Role of the Board," *Presidential Transition*, pp. 77–78.

- **Anticipate candidates' needs as well by putting in place a preliminary compensation range** and a performance assessment system.

- **To improve the board's own readiness to support a new president, conduct a self-assessment** and make necessary changes. In the competitive world of presidential searches, the board's preparation and behavior are critical to landing the best candidates.

Additional Articles from *Trusteeship*

Atwell, Robert and Barbara Wilson. "A Nontraditional President May Fit Just Right." *Trusteeship* (March/April 2003): pp. 24 – 28.

Carlson, Bryan E. and George J. Matthews. "Bridging the Leadership Gap." *Trusteeship* (May/June 2008): p. 27.

Ikenberry, Stanley O. "The Changing Demands of Presidential Leadership." *Trusteeship* (November/December 2010): p. 24.

Trachtenberg, Stephen Joel. "Reasonable Expectations of University Presidents." *Trusteeship* (March/April 2007): p. 13.

For more recommended reading, please see Resources at the end of this book.

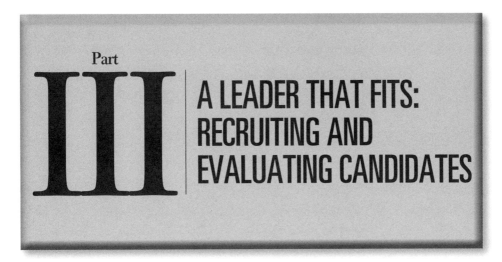

Part

III

A LEADER THAT FITS: RECRUITING AND EVALUATING CANDIDATES

Chapter 8

A Pool of Candidates

> **❝Creating a diverse candidate pool is a legal requirement for most presidential searches.❞**

ONCE THE PRESEARCH WORK has been completed—or, in the case of some tasks, is far enough along to ensure that its products will be available when needed—the search itself can commence. The main event, which everyone involved in the search has been waiting and preparing for, has arrived. The search begins with an effort to develop a roster of candidates who match the criteria set out in the position profile.

Now—usually a month to six weeks after receiving its charge from the board—the search committee and search consultant will shift into high gear. For the next six to eight weeks, a stepped-up effort will be necessary because recruiting must be an active process. Some institutions make the costly assumption that it will be enough to announce the vacancy. In fact, colleges and universities need to reach out aggressively and make their case if they want to access and engage the interest of the best candidates. Doing this enlists the efforts of many people, both on campus and off. The committee's task will be to orchestrate these efforts while focusing attention on the defined criteria.

SCOPE OF THE SEARCH

How wide a net should be cast? The precise answer depends on the circumstances, including the institution's mission, needs, traditions, and aspirations. But, unless restricted by charter or tradition, most colleges and universities will seek the benefits of a comprehensive search: broad outreach to various constituencies, a diverse group of candidates, and the best person for the job. Board members, for example, want not just a competent chief executive, but also the best match for their particular institution at this point in its history. They want the individual who most completely displays the leadership qualities they have carefully chosen.

Creating a diverse candidate pool is a legal requirement for most presidential searches, but it should also be an institutional imperative. The best person available may be, for example, female, African-American, Hispanic, a person with a disability, or a member of another group underrepresented in the ranks of college presidents. The last several decades have shown incontrovertibly that strong leadership has neither gender nor ethnic restrictions, nor ones related to sexual orientation or disability. Many members of formerly excluded groups have now attained levels of experience and accomplishment that qualify them as presidential candidates. One of the advantages of a comprehensive search is the opportunity to tap these reservoirs of talent.

Still another benefit of the broad search is the involvement of greater numbers of people. If invited to submit nominations or to suggest nominators, faculty, students, alumni, and local citizens gain a sense of participation and a stake in the outcome. Requests to educators, foundation officers, and other leaders arouse their interest in the institution, increase their knowledge of it, and, if made astutely, enhance its reputation.

Professional search consultants confirm the wisdom of casting a wide net. Because talent is broadly dispersed throughout the academic and other populations, it is impossible to predict where the best candidates will be found or how they will present themselves. No single route leads to the best candidates. The most productive searches do not limit themselves to a single means; they use all available means and use them aggressively.

Consultants do not, however, understand large as indiscriminate. A pool's size should not be increased for the sake of size alone. If the leadership criteria are well drawn, they will encourage better-qualified candidates who know by the careful wording that the search is a serious one. They will also discourage some (not all, unfortunately!) clearly unqualified candidates who apply for any new position, especially if the criteria are vague. Most search committees now issue a detailed prospectus, require a substantive and responsive letter of application, and take other measures designed to discourage casual applications.

Numbers can deceive. Two hundred candidates are not necessarily better than one hundred. An institution is, after all, looking for a single individual. What really counts is attracting 15 to 20 strong, plausible candidates who include among them 8 to 10 semifinalists and 3 to 5 finalists who are so impressive that the board will have genuine difficulty in choosing among them. To reach those final numbers, a large university or one that is nationally known may attract 50 to 100 candidates. Smaller institutions, especially specialized or regional ones, might develop a pool half as large but, if clear about the leadership criteria, could easily attract a better ratio of good finalists to total applicants than larger institutions.

It is worth remembering that, past a relatively early point in the search, it will be far easier to reduce the pool than enlarge it. A candidate who is in the pool can always be rejected; a potential candidate who is not in the pool cannot even be considered. In general, a larger, more diverse pool is always to an institution's advantage.

SOURCES OF NAMES

The three basic ways to develop a pool of candidates are: advertisements, calls for nominations, and direct recruitment. Most searches employ more than one of these means; many use all three and find the methods reinforce one another.

Advertisements

The position announcement—based on the position profile and prepared by the search consultant or search committee—can be brief or extensive depending on the institution's human resources requirements, its search budget, and the committee's view of what will be effective.[23] The ad should include submission information and requirements and state that the committee seeks not only applications but also nominations.

Well-placed ads can reach a large audience and generate a large volume of ap-

---

[23] Dowdall, *Searching for Higher Education Leadership*, p. 102.

plications, but usually they do not yield large numbers of competitive candidates. A few applicants, however, may hear about the vacancy from an ad, and the advertising enables an institution to reach out both widely and to specific audiences.

An advertising plan might include the following outlets:

- The institution's websites and appropriate publications, notably the campus newspaper or alumni magazine;
- National, regional, and local newspapers;
- Professional publications such as the *Chronicle of Higher Education*, *Inside Higher Ed*, and *Higher Ed Jobs*;
- Websites such as Diversejobs.net and publications like *Journal of Blacks in Higher Education*, *Hispanic Outlook on Higher Education*, and *Women in Higher Education*; and
- Publications and websites related to institutional type, religious affiliation, or other characteristics.

Advertising should keep the search highly visible over a month or so. An early start will be needed on ads to appear in print, especially national professional publications, as they may have lead times of several months.

Calls for Nominations

Nominations by knowledgeable individuals are among the very best sources of candidates. The extent of the outreach will depend on the national or regional character of the institution, the availability of funds, the breadth of the institution's network, and the concern committee members have for canvassing the field. Search consultants build and maintain extensive networks and can activate them on behalf of their clients. Aggressive outreach greatly increases the odds of robust results.

By letter or email, the search committee—primarily through the search consultant—will contact a wide network of potential nominators. These individuals should include people within higher education who have had opportunities to work with and appraise the promise of many professionals, as well as others outside the field, such as foundation officers, church leaders, government officials, heads of educational groups, collaborating organizations, professional associations, and selected friends of the college or university. Not to be overlooked are presidents and board members of peer institutions, which might include colleges ranked just below and just above the searching institution. Remember that the pool will be far less diverse if the call for nominations does not reach out to sources at minority-serving institutions.

It is wise not to skimp on this form of outreach because many of the best individuals—often the very best—are unlikely to respond to an advertisement. One may believe that an application suggests too much eagerness, another that her cause would be best served by a third party's introduction. Others are happily situated where they are, and some may be so modest as to think applying to your institution presumptuous. A nomination that puts a name into play—or even a suggestion that a person be contacted—can start a process that ends with a new, declared candidate.

Direct Recruitment

In direct recruitment, the search committee and especially the search consultant draw on existing networks and build new ones. The focus is on identifying, making contact with, and persuading potential candidates themselves. Of the three methods, this is the most laborious and time-consuming. It is also the most productive in the important sense that it typically produces a disproportionate share of serious contenders.

Many of the best potential future leaders probably are happily and successfully leading other organizations. With little or no intention or reason to look elsewhere, they need to be found, alerted to the opportunity, and given a reason to contemplate the possibility of a change. Other potential candidates might at some level know that they are ready to go elsewhere but be in no hurry to do so. They often have enough self-regard to expect that jobs will seek them rather than the reverse. The value of direct recruitment is that it can entice such candidates who may then consent to be nominated. The ideal candidate, in any case, may well be one who has a good position and substantial achievements but who can be persuaded to ask himself or herself, "Shall I stay here longer or go on to a different kind of challenge?"

The often-delicate and sometimes drawn-out process of courting likely candidates is the heart of direct recruitment, both at this beginning stage and later when the

WHEN DIRECT RECRUITMENT WORKS BEST

In response to a call for nominations by an independent university searching for a president, a highly respected academic leader—the provost at another institution—recommended someone she believed would make an excellent candidate. When the search consultant called to talk about the nomination, he asked the provost if she herself might be interested in the position. She hadn't given thought to leaving her current job, so she asked for time to consider the flattering offer.

After two more conversations with the consultant, she warmed to the prospect of making a change and taking on a new opportunity. She agreed to enter the search. After the usual sequence of interviews and campus visits, she was selected as president. Traditional advertising would not have resonated with this candidate who simply wasn't looking for a new position and was more focused on thinking of others who might be good candidates. Without the search consultant's direct recruitment efforts, she most likely would not have entered the search.

committee is nearing the moment of truth. Unfortunately, some possible candidates simply want to be courted. A committee should be wary of spending too much time on accomplished, prestigious candidates who are interesting but who do not show serious interest in the position.

Search consultants typically are hired for their contributions to direct recruiting. They and colleagues at their firms not only have extensive networks of potential nominators but also maintain ties with, know personally, or have reasonably reliable knowledge of large numbers of professionals who might be strong candidates. They know how to identify and approach still others who might prove to be. They are practiced at presenting opportunities to such individuals and asking them to consider them while providing straight answers to their questions. Not least important, their firms are set up to deal in an organized fashion with the large volumes of communication and highly individual approaches that direct recruitment entails. They use the personal connections of board and committee members as appropriate (if they know a prospect, the case is strong for their making the contact), while committee members coordinate their outreach closely with the consultant.

Direct recruitment requires an extensive but reasonably targeted list. A committee or consultant will need to bring existing contacts to the table but then generate many more. Begin by "ruling in" for possible contact individuals in certain categories, which might include: individuals at peer institutions (defined by size, level of instruction, control, mission, selectivity, and the like); presidents, vice presidents, deans, and others in positions where likely candidates might be found; and individuals already in the region (perhaps less salient in today's highly mobile professional market). Remember to include categories associated with diversity—historically African American or Hispanic-serving institutions, for example. To accommodate interest in candidates with nontraditional backgrounds—business, government, nonprofits, the military, the professions—one or more of those sectors might become categories. One aim is to see, as student admissions professionals say, how many circles can be drawn around a prospect. Those who can be identified as belonging to more sought-after categories than others might merit the most attention.

Direct recruitment may initially involve mailing and emailing, but establishing contact with potential candidates requires extensive cold calling, with follow-up conversations when discovering an openness to hear more. Working one's list can be tedious and is certainly one of the less glamorous parts of the process. But from time to time, a promising nugget appears in the prospector's pan. Then, possibly more than at any other time in the search, the skill and experience of the institutional spokesperson (usually in this work the consultant) can make a difference to the outcome of the whole project. The abilities to understand a strong prospect's professional situation, listen to his or her concerns, and deftly present the opportunities offered by a new institution can make all the difference in the quality of a final applicant pool.

With some strong candidates, the search committee chair or the board chair should make the overture. There may be a case for some gentle indirection, unusual flexibility, or other tailored strategy with these individuals. Sometimes committees create an obstacle for themselves, for example, by asking people who have been nominated or whom they have identified as especially promising whether they are interested in applying for the job. A better approach may be to ask if the committee can interest them in the position or whether the committee might talk with them about possible candidates. Out of this conversation might develop a person's own interest in being considered.

Similarly, it may be best to forego a hard deadline for applications from these "reach" candidates and instead to give a date when application review will begin.[24] A strong candidate may, for fear of disclosure, want to minimize the period when his or her name is in play and therefore submit at the last possible moment. From time to time search committees may also depart dramatically from their playbooks by, for example, inviting a particularly desirable candidate to campus for a private conversation or having the board or committee chair pay him or her a personal visit. Consistency may have its virtues, these committees calculate, but is not an absolute good. If these kinds of special steps are necessary to find a truly exceptional next president, they are well worth taking.

A SYSTEM FOR HANDLING RESPONSES

Efforts to develop a pool of candidates, it is hoped, will generate a large number of applications, nominations, suggestions, and inquiries, all of which will need to be received, recorded, and acknowledged according to an efficient system. For searches assisted by a consultant, the contract will specify how the committee and the consultant will divide the work at this point. Some consultants will want only applications prompted through their calls for nomination and direct recruitment efforts sent to them; the rest will go to the search committee.[25] But most committees and consultants will prefer that the search firm handle all applications and nominations, subject to the committee's oversight and policies. Firms are typically well equipped for this work, and entrusting them with it frees the committee—and especially the chair—for other tasks.

Developing a pool is critical work—not sufficient for success but absolutely necessary. It creates real-life applicants and plausible candidates that can generate real excitement and unanticipated possibilities. The sometimes tedious work of advertising, seeking nominations, and direct recruitment pays off soon enough. It creates a momentum that carries the process forward into its next stage where candidates are given a series of progressively closer looks and their ranks are reduced to a select, competitive few.

---

[24] Ibid., pp. 112–13.

[25] Ibid., p. 103.

Key Points

- **Decide the scope of the search.** A comprehensive national effort that generates a diverse candidate pool will increase the odds of finding the best person available.

- **Reach out broadly with a combination of advertising, soliciting nominations, and direct recruiting** to generate a robust group of talented candidates.

- **Direct recruitment,** to which search consultants have much to contribute, produces the largest share of serious and viable contenders for the presidency.

Chapter 9

Identifying Semifinalists

> **"...the initial review of applications is generally regarded as a committee responsibility."**

THE EXCITEMENT BUILDS when the search committee sees the first fruits of its labors in the form of actual applications. Committee members often have high hopes that something very good awaits—and in most cases, it does. But predictably, the work is just beginning. Next, the committee will screen the truly promising applicants from the not-so-promising. It identifies a short list of 12 to 15 candidates for more serious consideration and then selects 6 to 8 semifinalists, typically for interviews at a neutral, off-campus site. *(See Chapter 10.)*

This process will depend largely on whether a search consultant has been retained and, if so, what arrangements the committee has made regarding division of labor. As in other parts of the process, the committee must make its best effort to complete the tasks that are not within the consultant's scope.

INITIAL SCREENING

Applications will be processed and posted promptly on the search committee's secure, password-protected website. Although some search committees may ask a search firm to take sole responsibility for screening applications (and, in some cases, even for bringing them the five to 10 most competitive candidates), the initial review of applications is generally regarded as a committee responsibility, often with consultant coordination. Depending on the numbers involved and other factors, each member may read each application, a subcommittee may read them, or the applications may be divided among subgroups. The consultant will in most cases review all applications as well, providing a professional second opinion. Ultimately—often at the committee's third or fourth meeting—all judgments will be presented and discussed.

Practice Evaluation Meeting

First, however, at a meeting held face-to-face or by phone, the committee or subcommittee should practice its evaluation techniques. Working through and screening applications together will help ensure consistency and give committee members confidence, individually and collectively, that they are ready for the task.

The committee chair and consultant should prepare a candidate ratings guide that directly reflects the criteria set out in the position profile. *(See Appendix F for a sample ratings guide.)* Using two or three sample applications—selected because they raise key issues that may arise in screening—committee members will rank candidates according to how well they meet the criteria. This practice session is also a good time to remind members about their obligation to keep names confidential and—to minimize inappropriate influences—the importance of not talking among themselves about individual candidacies.

Initial Screening Meeting

The goal of this meeting is to winnow the pool down to a short list of 12 to 15 candidates, more or less. Each person on the list must possess genuine promise as a future leader of the institution. Although an initial cut could be made on the password-protected website, a face-to-face meeting will be more instructive for all and generally produces more considered results. When the search committee meets to discuss the candidates, members will bring completed ratings guides for each candidate. The discussion, typically led by the consultant or search committee chair, can be structured in a variety of ways. Sometimes readers are asked to come to the meeting with a list of their top 10 candidates, and the lists are then compared. One simple, proven approach is first to ask readers to divide applicants into "yes," "no," and "maybe" groups according to whether they want to explore their candidacies further. An initial tally will usually reveal extensive agreement about those who can at this point be thanked and those who are of genuine interest.

If subgroups are used (so that, say, five teams each read and evaluate one-fifth of the applications submitted), extra care should be taken to ensure that all teams use uniform standards of judgment. If any anxiety lingers that teams are using different standards, the chair can review all dossiers to ensure conformity. This additional step can help address another occasional concern—that if one or more of the teams do not include a board member, the board's responsibility for selection may in some way be compromised.

It is an enduring curiosity to those familiar with presidential searches that so many applications are so far off the mark. The candidates behind them often lack the specified degree or level of education or have limited relevant experience. Some seem not to have read the position profile. Others present themselves haplessly. The good news is that a clear majority of candidates can usually be quickly and easily eliminated from serious consideration.

By contrast, some "maybes" will be well worth discussing. Some members may have information or perspective on an individual that, once shared, will make him or her a clear "yes" or "no." Or the committee may decide that it needs to learn more about an applicant and will carry him or her forward, for the time being, at least as an alternate.

To help committee members identify a short list of 12 to 15 candidates, the consultant can begin to bring information about particular ones to the group. He or she may have information gleaned from previous searches that can be shared. Moreover, a consultant will have been working quietly for a month or more, contacting and speaking with the most promising applicants and nominees—assessing interest and potential, and encouraging nominees who have not yet submitted applications to apply.

FOLLOW-UP STEPS

The committee should ensure that it communicates with all candidates about their status. Most will be thanked again warmly for their interest but told that their candidacies will not be pursued further. The search's public website should be updated at this time with news of the committee's progress, including some general statistics about the pool of candidates it has worked with, and perhaps more current detail on the nature and timing of the next steps.

The 12 to 15 short-listed candidates are the most important among those to be updated on their status. They should be congratulated, asked to confirm their continuing interest, and given an opportunity to ask any questions they might have. The committee should communicate three important pieces of information:

- **Dates:** The candidates should be told to hold the dates set for off-campus interviews.

- **Reference checks:** The committee should request candidates' permission to call their references and ask them to tell their references to expect calls. They should also receive a clear explanation that deeper reference and background checks lie ahead for semifinalists and finalists and an indication of the point at which candidacies will no longer be kept confidential.

- **Compensation:** The search committee chair or search consultant asks each candidate about his or her compensation—current and expected. As the likely compensation range for the position is discussed, some candidates may decide to withdraw now—not an ideal development, but better than having them drop out later in the process because they were not told compensation information. Others may become still more interested, and in many cases, information will be gleaned from candidates that helpfully informs negotiations later in the process.

REFERENCE CALLS AND FURTHER CHECKS

With the short list of candidates identified and informed of their status, some reference calls and further checks are in order. This work—which will be done with more and more thoroughness as the search proceeds—provides at this point a basis for narrowing the short list to a smaller group of six to eight semifinalists who will be invited to a first round of interviews at a neutral site.

Although the committee or search firm may have done a preliminary online search on selected candidates before creating the short list, now is the time for a somewhat expanded check using a standard search engine and tools like Wikipedia. A candidate's presence, if any, on social media (for example, LinkedIn, Facebook, and Twitter) will be of interest. The purpose of this research is to help the committee learn more about the candidates as they, others, and the public record present them. More careful scrutiny will await those who advance further, but the effort to prevent surprises should by this point be well underway.

Systematic telephone conversation with all listed references is a critical line of work in presidential searches. The calls begin here, before the committee's fourth or fifth meeting. Here, as so often in the process of search, a choice must be made. Will the consultant make all the calls and then report the results to the committee? This approach can ensure a high degree of consistency and artfulness in the questioning, along with an astute processing of the information gathered. But it may cause the committee to be more dependent than it wishes to be on the consultant's perspective and to question input that has been filtered through one set of ears. Checking references is a powerful way to develop a personal feel for candidates, and search committees may want to seize this opportunity as much as possible. The consultant will not have the time to complete 60 to 75 full reference calls in a week or two, especially when he or she may be serving multiple clients at the same time. Instead, these calls will likely be turned over to junior staff.

Most committees will divide the calls, with five or six per member made over a two-week period. Several factors come into play when making the assignments. A different caller is assigned to each one of a candidate's references so that various members hear about the candidate. To encourage candor and comfort, each reference is matched with a caller he or she regards as a peer, and committee members are assigned to call references they already know.

Speaking with references requires considerable skill—more than some committee members are likely to possess. The committee should provide training. With the help of a consultant, members agree on a protocol of questions reflecting the position profile. This strategy focuses callers on the most productive and appropriate questions and discourages them from wandering

> **❝ The consultant will not have the time to complete 60 to 75 full reference calls in a week or two.❞**

off into the wrong territory. It also warns them of questions never to ask, such as those having to do with race, national origin, disability, age, sexual orientation, and other protected class characteristics set out in the institution's non-discrimination statement.

Adherence to this framework will also be helpful when it comes time to compare candidates. Callers should, however, be able to tailor questions somewhat to particular candidates and follow up with unscripted ones when something emerges that could be important.

References can be surprisingly helpful when the conversation is not just about the virtues of the candidate (who may after all be a friend or someone to whom the reference feels some loyalty) but about how well he or she matches up with the institution and its particular set of needs. The reference is in this case free to be candid.

WINNOWING THE LIST

Callers record the significant points of each call on reference report forms, which are shared with the committee when it reconvenes for its fourth or fifth meeting—generally a couple of weeks after choosing the short list. At this meeting, the committee hears reference reports and then selects six to eight semifinalists. This will be the longest of all search committee meetings and with good reason. It marks the point when the committee must make tough decisions about what it is really seeking. If a consultant assists, he or she likely provides important background and perspective. Robust discussion is in order and members may disagree. If so, a committee may want to err on the side of carrying a candidate forward. Many candidates overcome initial concerns as a search proceeds and, as their strengths become apparent, more than a few of these are chosen. Not everyone the committee advances may decide to continue, so there may well be room for an alternate or two on the roster.

The selection of the six to eight semifinalists is another good occasion to post an update on the search's public site. No names will be disclosed. But the update can describe the interest of so many in helping the institution, the continuing interest of those on the short list, and the committee's good progress in carefully selecting among them. Meanwhile, those not selected should be thanked promptly for their interest, time and cooperation, and at least summary records of all reference calls and online checks should be retained electronically as part of the search's files.

Key Points

- **Using a common approach, reduce the pool of candidates to a short list of 12 to 15** and then, through further reference checks and discussion, to 6 to 8 semifinalists.

- **A yes-no-maybe rating system is a useful tool** for initial ranking. Committees often find the "maybes" worth discussing and learning more about.

- **Seeking consensus instead of taking votes promotes discussion** and information sharing among committee members.

- **References may feel they can be more candid when asked not about a candidate generally** but about how well he or she would match up with the institution's particular needs.

Chapter 10

Interviews and the Selection of Finalists

> **"Interviewing is a fine art that not everyone possesses by nature or experience. "**

S CREENING CANDIDATES on the basis of their written credentials and calls to references is the first step in sorting through the candidate pool. Interviewing those who survive—the semifinalists—is the second. In this essential stage of the search, candidates and search committee members have their first opportunity for face-to-face interaction and mutual questioning. Interviews can strongly confirm or fundamentally transform impressions formed to this point. These experiences are often decisive—sometimes even more than they should be. As the primary means of appraising the semifinalists for the presidency, the interviews deserve careful planning.

PREPARING THE CANDIDATES

The search committee chair or search consultant should write to the advancing candidates immediately after their selection as semifinalists, formally notifying them of their status and offering congratulations. For a more personal interaction, he or she should also call the semifinalists and confirm interest in participating in the next phase. The candidates should already have the interview dates set aside, and they should now be put in touch with the individual at the institution or the search firm who will coordinate the logistics of their travel and lodging. Candidates' expenses should be covered. Spouses or partners are not customarily included at the first interview but, if invited, their expenses should also be paid.

The chair or consultant will also want to explore the candidates' involvements in any other searches and—another sometimes delicate matter—ask whether the committee should be prepared for anything that might come to light in further background checks.

The candidates should also receive additional information on the college or university. Materials to be sent might include:

- The last several president's reports;
- A summary of the strategic plan;
- A summary of recent accreditation reports;
- Financial statements;
- Overviews of student recruitment and retention;
- A current summary of fundraising efforts and results;
- Recent issues of the alumni magazine; and
- A list of search committee members.

Among other purposes, sharing these documents gives candidates important information about the institution's weaknesses and challenges. Newly appointed presidents regularly complain that they lacked truly relevant information about the people and problems of an institution before they made a decision about the job. This lack of disclosure can naturally cause resentment later. It no doubt has contributed to individuals taking jobs when they were not prepared to cope with the challenges and to skillful practitioners turning down jobs that they might have felt differently about had they understood the challenges better.

Finally, secure each candidate's permission to contact some additional references before or immediately after the interviews. These individuals may not be limited to those the candidate suggests, but the candidate should be told who might be called in the weeks leading up the interview. Often the best sources are those mentioned by references in the first phase of calling. The search committee chair should again assure the candidate that, beyond making these contacts, the search will keep his or her participation in strict confidence and should tell the candidate to remind these references to do so as well. The idea at this stage is that the candidate is kept closely apprised of who is to be called, even though the circle may be widening beyond the names originally provided.

THE INTERVIEW FORMAT

Some time and effort should go toward preparing those who will conduct the interviews. Although sometimes only a subset of the search committee meets with the semifinalists, it is preferable for the entire group to participate, or at least be present. This practice helps ensure that each member has the same information about each candidate, facilitates consensus, and makes a better impression on those interviewed. Interviewing, however, is a fine art that not everyone possesses by nature or experience. Most committee members—generally even those who think of themselves as quite proficient—will profit from professional guidance. A training session or a practice run under the supervision of the search consultant may greatly improve performance.

The consultant or search committee chair should also draft a set of interview questions, including a core group that go to key aspects of the position profile. It will be especially important to compare candidates' leadership qualities with those set out in the position profile and learn of their concrete experience dealing with the types of challenges the institution faces and their ideas for addressing them. Questions may touch on any or all of a wide range of topics, including:

- Institutional mission;
- Leadership and planning experience;
- Academic vision;
- Board, faculty, alumni, and community relations;
- Fundraising;
- Management style;
- Student life; and
- Candidate concerns and questions.

Once the committee has had a chance to suggest revisions and the questions have been approved, the plan should be to ask them of every candidate.

Many searches gain additional persuasive firepower by having the board chair meet separately with the candidates at the interview site. This opportunity helps give each candidate a sense of the individual to whom he or she would most likely report (and vice versa). The additional time also allows the chair to help candidates understand fully the attractiveness of the institution and the position. If this course is taken, the committee should think through in advance what role, if any, to give the chair in its debriefing meeting. Some committees prefer restricting this meeting to committee members alone, while others see value in gauging the board chair's feelings about candidates with whom he or she will need to form a significant working relationship. [26]

Focusing on the leadership qualities sought will provide comparability among interviews and consistency in the committee's inquiries. But each individual's record will offer a distinctive context for the conversation and present its own blank spots or ambiguous areas that require clarification. This argues for tailoring the interviews to the individuals where possible. (It may not be at many public institutions.) The art of interviewing involves thinking about each interviewee in advance and designing questions that will exhibit the strengths and weaknesses, professional competence, and human qualities of the candidate. Some tailoring of the questions to each candidate shows that the committee is well prepared and gives the candidate a sense that this is truly a personal interview. The committee should agree on the form of these adjustments, and then each question should be assigned to a specific committee member.

TIMING

As mentioned in Chapter 6, early in the process, the search committee should identify the specific dates, times, and lengths of all its meetings, including the days it will set aside for neutral-site interviews and for finalists' campus interviews. Since both committee members and short-listed candidates know the search's timeline, it should be possible to schedule the neutral-site interviews within ten days of the selection and notification of semifinalists. These interviews will constitute the search committee's fifth or sixth meeting and occur late in the third or early in the fourth month of the search. For six to eight candidates, two full days should be set aside.

---

[26] Ibid., pp. 122–23.

The search committee chair or consultant should give candidates a detailed interview schedule as soon as possible. As a matter of courtesy and confidentiality, the schedule should be arranged so that candidates do not encounter one another—a challenge that will require minute-by-minute planning. Even when the semifinalist list is public knowledge, candidates should be kept out of one another's way.

An hour and a half per candidate is a reasonable allocation of time. It allows for the committee to pose 10 to 20 questions and for the candidate to ask his or her own questions. Before a candidate appears, the committee chair or consultant will have time to review briefly with the committee basic information about his or her background, information gleaned from references, and concerns that might be explored. At the conclusion of each interview, time is needed for making notes and giving instructions to the group. Three (or at most four) interviews are enough for one day.

At the end of the two days, the committee may want to set aside time for group discussion of each candidate. Until then, they may want to agree not to discuss the interviewees. Views shift during the course of interviews, and airing individual assessments can freeze the development of additional perspectives.

LOCATION

Confidentiality is best served by selecting a neutral, off-campus site for the interviews. A major airport generally serves well, as it has access to transportation, lodging, food, and well-equipped meeting space. But searches sometimes employ, for example, a nearby hotel, a board member's office, or a corporate meeting room. Community colleges are more inclined to hold interviews on campus. For many of them, confidentiality is less important than convenience, and, in some states, everything is done out in the open under the requirements of sunshine laws.

The physical setting of the interviews should be appropriate, tasteful, and pleasant. Some thought needs to be given to the room in which the interviews take place and to the placing of chairs and tables to create an informal and, so far as possible, relaxed atmosphere. Interior rooms with no windows become oppressive to candidates and committees alike. If candidates are to be kept waiting, a pleasant and relatively private place to wait is important.

SOME COMMON MISSTEPS

Most search committee members will have had experience interviewing candidates for positions within or outside of the academic world. That experience—combined with some training and group planning and with their own common sense about human nature and group dynamics—will go far toward ensuring that the interviews will be productive and give the committee a much better understanding of the candidates. But committees tend to make some common mistakes when interviewing candidates. Discussion of these potential missteps should be a part of preliminary training and planning.

Forgetting that the Candidate Is Auditioning the Institution

Committee members have the difficult role of being both questioners and salespeople. At this initial interview stage, the candidate is judging the college or university just as the committee is appraising the candidate. These meetings are usually the first face-to-face contact between the candidates and the committee after weeks of correspondence, telephone conversations, and waiting. The impressions gained on both sides are often crucial.

The best candidates often are skeptical but interested and want more information. They will be influenced by the way they are treated, the questions they are asked and how theirs are answered, and the setting and atmosphere of the interview. Thoughtful candidates may have conducted a surprising amount of research on the institution on their own and will ask about matters like these:

- The institution's operations, along with its problems and prospects;
- The extent to which board members, faculty, and others understand the challenges and opportunities, as well as the degree of their commitment to the institution;
- In a public college or university, the state of the political climate and the influence of the governor's office, the legislative committee on education, and the budget system;
- How the board engages in the strategic issues facing the institution; and
- How well shared governance is conducted.

Rather than resenting inquiries by candidates, committees should welcome them. Requests for information or frank opinions are, after all, promising signs of engagement, and the eventual fit the committee seeks can only be achieved in an atmosphere of candid exchange.

From the committee's side of the table, the interview is a perfect occasion not only to answer questions, but to present the institution's presidency as an attractive opportunity. Every committee member should be prepared to answer the questions most likely to be raised (at least at a basic level) and also to make the case for each candidate to seriously consider the position. The committee chair will in most cases play the lead role here. In conducting the interviews he or she generally should strive to put each candidate at ease, direct the course of the discussion, curb irrelevancies, stop the undiplomatic committee member, and ease any embarrassing situations with humor or a change of topic.

Relying on First Impressions

An interview is not the best predictor of an individual's success in a presidency. One candidate may arrive with a history at prestigious universities and the style and apparent acuity to match. Another may offer a particularly winning personality. A third may show an impressive facility for prescribing solutions to your institution's problems. But, while these characteristics and traits could all be helpful, none should be mistaken for a full readiness to be an effective president, as defined by a thorough position description. *A candidate's record of achievements is the main indicator.*

Effective search committees keep their guards up to a degree, wary of succumbing hastily to any candidate's charms. They do not discard a candidate too quickly if he or she does not make an overwhelming first impression but has a solid record. This candidate may grow on the committee as his or her true strengths gradually are revealed. Essentially, astute committee members use the interview to supplement—to extend and deepen—what is learned from other sources, not to supplant it. Grounding the conversation in concrete instances of a candidate's past performance when confronted with relevant challenges often sheds the light needed.

Missing the Opportunity to Confirm Interests and Intentions

Take some time at the interviews for confidential conversation between the search committee chair or consultant (or the board chair, if applicable) and each candidate. Confirm the individual's continuing interest in the position—whether you can count on his or her participation if selected as a finalist. Also, get a sense of what, if any, particular issues might need to be addressed if he or she is selected to receive an offer. Neutral-site interviews are the time to share this kind of information and confirm interest and intentions in ways that help minimize unexpected attrition in the candidate pool. It is also an appropriate time to ask for an update on each candidate's participation in other searches. The search committee's policy regarding the eventual disclosure of candidate's names should be reviewed again to avoid surprises. Finally, candidates should receive at this point a basic outline of the likely contract and compensation.

Rushing to Judgment

Immediately following each interview, committee members should record their individual impressions. Whether they rely on a previously agreed-upon rating sheet or their own scribbled notes, they should record their reactions to the strengths and weaknesses of the candidates promptly. With six or eight individuals being compared, it is easy to become forgetful or uncertain. The written record becomes invaluable.

Many search committees then hold a debriefing meeting before ranking the candidates. Once the interviews are completed, it is tempting to rush to judgment. A danger is that one, two, or three very outspoken—and typically powerful—committee members will pronounce their opinions and preferences in a way that effectively shuts down discussion, regardless of the merits of the candidates or the range of opinions in the group. Better initially for all members to quickly review together what has been learned about each interviewee in turn—establishing facts about what each said and didn't, what issues might need further exploration, and other factors—than to turn immediately to comparisons. Having a brief, nonjudgmental review before ranking candidates can help prevent this perversion of the process.

> 66 **An interview is not the best predictor of an individual's success in a presidency. A candidate's record of achievements is the main indicator.** 99

WRAPPING UP AND MOVING FORWARD

More likely than not, the early vetting and interviews will generate considerable consensus—positive and negative—about several candidates, including two to four who garner unanimous support. While the committee should follow a process to some degree, there is no need to hold lengthy discussions about each of the other candidates. Focus on those who have considerable but not yet full support. Consider all the evidence—letters, CVs, background checks, and reference calls, as well as the interviews just completed.

A top set of three or four finalists should soon emerge. In most searches, they will be invited to make campus visits. Usually a campus cannot pay adequate attention to visits by more than four finalists, so that number is a good outer limit. It is often wise to choose an alternate because at this time, more than at other points in the search, one or more candidates may withdraw. If there is a large pool of finalists or if candidates face the prospect of their participation being publicly disclosed as the search culminates, some (especially sitting presidents) may have second thoughts. Inviting four or five—from whom three or four might accept—tends to be safe.

As was the case when semifinalists were selected, it is important to notify immediately all those who are not chosen and thank them warmly for their participation in the process. If the committee must defer its decisions pending completion of other interviews or collection of more information, let the candidates know when they will hear further word. Consistent with the communications plan and the policy regarding disclosure or nondisclosure of candidates' identities, the search's spokesperson should also announce to the public the important milestone that has been reached. The search's public website, for example, might be updated to reflect the fact that several as-yet-unnamed finalists have been chosen and that their identities and plans for them to visit campus will soon be announced.

Key Points

- **Before interviews, prepare candidates with thorough information** and committee members with training and practice.

- **Attend closely to the logistics of the interview.** Be sensitive to candidates' needs for confidentiality.

- **Avoid common mistakes**—for example, putting too much emphasis on impressions made in the interview, failing to "sell" the opportunity to candidates, and neglecting to confirm candidates' interest and address any concerns they might have.

- **Select the top four candidates** (and perhaps an alternate) to invite for on-campus interviews.

Chapter 11

Due Diligence

> **❝ No matter who is responsible, background check due diligence is of the greatest importance. ❞**

A FTER THE FIELD NARROWS to three to four finalists, most committees face two assignments. The first, the subject of this chapter, is to complete the investigation of the candidates to obtain as much information as possible on each person's background and performance. The second, addressed in the next chapter, is to expose them and the college or university community to one another to find out how compatible and enthusiastic they are after closer acquaintance and inspection. In a sense, the campus visit is one more step—usually the last—in checking out the candidate. It also gives finalists a chance to gain a much better sense of the institution.

COMMUNICATING WITH FINALISTS

The search committee wants to make the best possible impression on the finalists, so it is critical to work out logistics, have a plan in place to support them, and extend the institution's hospitality. The necessary starting point for the final checks and reference calls is a letter and follow-up call from the search committee chair to each finalist (and any alternates) immediately after the neutral-site interviews. In this communication, the finalists should be congratulated for advancing and asked to reconfirm their participation in the next phase.

Confirmed finalists should be notified of the dates of the campus visits as well as the name and contact information of the individual who will assist them with travel and lodging arrangements. If the candidate has a spouse or partner, he or she should also be invited. In some searches, children are welcomed as well.

The final candidates should receive additional materials on the institution that will help them further understand the college or university and prepare for their conversations on campus. *(See Appendix E.)* These materials might provide more detailed views of the institution's operations and performance over several years. Include budgets and audits, fundraising history, enrollment history—all showing projected and actual figures, by category. Data from national surveys might be appropriate—for example, the National Survey of Student Engagement and the CIRP Freshman Survey from the Higher Education Institute. Institutional data from senior and alumni surveys, self-studies, and consultants' reports may also be useful. Share anything—including information about institutional stresses and failures—that will be relevant and helpful. Be ready to provide further information if requested.

FINAL BACKGROUND CHECKS

At this stage, finalists undergo an exhaustive background check that extends well beyond the kind of Internet search conducted earlier in the process. The search committee or search consultant should tell each candidate to expect forms that authorize and enable this step. When, and only when, this paperwork is returned, the background check should be carried out. It should explore any criminal record and involvement in legal cases. It should provide verification of the individual's employment and credit history. Military and department of motor vehicles records should be consulted. Degrees should be confirmed. Any claimed record of publications should be carefully checked out. So should the individual's presence in the press and other media—notably social media. Questions raised at this stage are often easily and satisfactorily answered. Those that can't be will at least not have arisen too late.

The background check may be conducted by the search committee chair, perhaps with the assistance of the human resources office; by a search consultant (who may subcontract some of it to a firm specializing in this kind of work); or by a combination of the above. No matter who is responsible, this due diligence is of the greatest importance. Unfortunately it is not that unusual to find that a president—often well into his or her service—has a serious issue that should have come to light in a thorough background check. And too often one hears media reports on university leaders who have embellished their resumes. Usually, the misrepresentations were there all along but for whatever reason—carelessness, haste—remained undiscovered. The toll in such cases can be crushingly heavy, not only in personal and professional terms for the president, but also in terms of institutional embarrassment, loss of board credibility, tarnished reputations with institutional stakeholders, and damage to fundraising.

FINAL REFERENCE CHECKS

Like background checks, final reference checks are critically important. During the screening process, committees presumably contacted the references supplied by the candidates and, with the candidates' knowledge and approval, a number of others as well. If the references have been able to relate the individual's record to the position profile, and if they have been astutely probed, their testimony has already provided a base of valuable information. Now it is important to fill in the picture.

The committee will want to be in touch with people who have worked closely with the candidate in present and previous positions. These individuals should be able to give independent appraisals of the candidate's judgment and capacity to work with others, delegate responsibility, function under stress, and exemplify the qualities the committee is looking for in private as well as public life.

This work could be completed earlier. But in view of the disclosure and potential awkwardness that results from local investigations, it is better to hold off on unlimited inquiries until the list of candidates has been reduced to the finalists. And it is more efficient to limit deeper scrutiny to this smaller set.

At this point, the search committee chair or consultant should ask the candidates to permit them to call any individuals they may choose regarding the candidacies. In this final phase, all restrictions are off, and candidates should be so advised. Anyone

❝People the candidate has worked for may paint a different picture than those who have worked for the candidate. Performance in one job may differ markedly from performance in another. Some convey their views persuasively regardless of accuracy or insightfulness.❞

may—indeed, should—be contacted whose professional opinions about the candidates or experiences with them are germane. They in turn should be asked to suggest further sources. The candidate need no longer be advised who will be contacted.

Most candidates understandably might prefer to have this kind of home-base investigation deferred as late in the process as possible until after they have visited the campus and ascertained strong interest on both sides—or even until they have an offer. However, unless the next interviews are to be held close—conducted solely by the board, for example—this practice would be highly inconsistent with the institution's interests in presenting to the campus community and the public a thoroughly vetted field of finalists, each worthy of an offer. Most candidates therefore will agree to these calls, recognizing when local inquiries can no longer be postponed. For its part, the committee should make its calls with sensitivity and with the candidates' knowledge that anyone may be called. But if at this stage the candidate is still reluctant to have any inquiries made on his or her home campus, the committee should proceed with great caution, if at all. The failure to investigate thoroughly can be a fatal mistake.

Although most candidates grant permission for unrestricted reference calling—as they were apprised from the beginning that they would need to—the moment does call for some accommodation to individual situations. For the large majority of searches that use an open process for campus interviews, the candidates' cover is now blown. The chair will in most cases inform candidates that a bulletin announcing the finalists will be issued to the campus, followed almost immediately by a news release to the media, and that a brief biography will be prepared for public distribution and posting on the search's website. In response, some candidates may ask—quite reasonably—for a short delay before the announcement so that they can inform colleagues and trustees before the news appears in the media.

Final reference calls, like the earlier ones, benefit from preparation. The committee should design a series of remaining questions based on the position profile and on any issues about the candidate that need further probing. Callers should ask for clarification of ambiguities and be alert to implications. Even the reference's inflections and hesitations in answering questions can reveal helpful information. Before the call concludes, it is probably wise to ask for any information that could be damaging to the candidate. References will not ordinarily volunteer such information, but most recognize its importance and respond to an inquiry. To put the respondent at ease, the question might be approached indirectly; the caller might ask, for example, "If I were to visit your campus and talk with some people who dislike the candidate, what reservations might I hear?" This helps the respondent to answer objectively without feeling disloyal.

The harvest of information, judgments, opinions, and speculations these calls bring in must be interpreted with care. People the candidate has worked for may have a quite different picture from those who have worked for the candidate. Performance in one job may differ markedly from performance in another. One source will know a candidate intimately, the next not well at all. Some views are conveyed far more persuasively than others, regardless of their accuracy or insightfulness. The hostile critic needs to be discounted as much as the undiscriminating friend. Most strong candidates will have made *some* enemies. The final product will necessarily be a composite assessment, for no one sees the whole individual, and it may be a mixed one.

Callers should write a brief summary following each call while its nuances are still fresh in mind. When all calls have been completed, the summaries can be shared with other members of the committee, but under no circumstances should they go beyond that group. Even though the candidacy may already be public, respondents must be assured that their judgments will remain confidential.

Key Points

- **Advise candidates additional reference calls** may now be made to anyone.

- **Complete the investigation of the finalists** to obtain as much information as possible on their backgrounds and performance.

- **Overlooking this due diligence could have costly consequences** for the institution's reputation.

- **Final reference calls provide opportunities to clear up ambiguities** and ask remaining questions about the candidate. The results will need to be interpreted with care.

A Leader That Fits: Recruiting and Evaluating Candidates

Chapter 12
Final Interviews and the Committee's Recommendations

> **❝Steeped in the values of shared governance, few campuses welcome or honor a cloistered process.❞**

THE SEARCH FOR A NEW PRESIDENT now transitions from the final reference and background checks to the on-campus interviews and search committee recommendations. This is a big moment, as the committee's work approaches completion. But with it come important questions: What level of confidentiality applies here? How are campus visits organized, and who is involved? What should be done to welcome and assist spouses, partners, and families? What are the search committee's options in making recommendations to the board?

DECIDING ON THE OPENNESS OF THE FINAL INTERVIEWS

At virtually all public colleges and universities and most independent institutions, the final interviews are an open process, with the identities of candidates announced to the campus and external communities. This openness is strongly recommended.

Sometimes presidential searches do maintain secrecy to the very end through a more restricted or "closed" final phase. Candidates are brought anonymously onto campus or to a meeting place elsewhere, and they meet with a limited number of representatives of the community, in some cases only with the board. All participants are committed to complete confidentiality.

The usual rationale for closed searches is that the best candidates—especially sitting presidents—are often the least inclined to have their interest publicly disclosed or to submit to public scrutiny. *(See "Confidentiality," Chapter 6.)* Generally, search committees that forego an open process have one or more such candidates in their pool of finalists and lack confidence that they can make a satisfactory appointment without them.

When search committees do this, however, they are often forgetting or ignoring the many reasons for openness. The various campus constituencies will be eager to see what the candidates look like, what impression they make, whether they are educators or managers, scholars or fundraisers. *(See "Engaging Constituencies," later in this chapter.)* These constituencies want to feel they had some voice in the final selection, and they include many whose input could be valuable. Steeped in the values of shared governance, few campuses welcome or honor a cloistered process. Faculty members in particular can resent not being allowed a preview. Some may view this as deliberate indifference to their concerns and judgment and may feel alienated from (or even hostile toward) a new president they have never seen. No matter how outstanding, presidents must live and work productively with faculty, students, administrative officers, alumni, state education officials, and others. To be effective, they need the support of these powerful groups. The best way of ensuring the support of those groups at the start is by involving them in the selection.

Although some candidates will prefer continued confidentiality, most will want a campus visit. Unless they already are familiar with the campus, they will want to see its buildings, grounds, and location. They may want to get some measure of the faculty's concern for educational issues, the composition and quality of the student body, the structure and competence of the administrative staff, and the feelings these groups have for the institution. They will want to talk with the administrative officers with whom they would be working most closely. They may want to speak with the outgoing president for an assessment of the institution's future prospects. And they will surely see the board's openness or lack thereof in the search process as a telling indication of its values and ways of operating. What they find from an open visit may produce doubts or certainty that they are not interested; but just as often, if they were hesitant and skeptical at some level before the visit, they now find themselves strongly drawn to the opportunity. For all these reasons and more, most institutions doing searches now conduct campus visits openly.

For the search committee and the campus community, open campus visits are crucial in two further respects. First, they reveal things that no round of interviews or phone calls will reveal about candidates and how they will operate in the institution's environment. Many times, the search committee's ranking of finalists changes dramatically in the course of their successive visits. Second, if a candidate evokes a less-than-positive reaction—from lack of enthusiasm to outright dislike—from a member of the campus community (staff in the athletic department, a vice president, a key donor, or anyone else invited to participate in the visit), board members will want to know that fact *before* awarding the candidate a three-year

> 66 **No matter how outstanding, presidents must live and work productively with faculty, students, administrative officers, alumni, state education officials, and others. The best way of ensuring the support of those groups at the start is by involving them in the selection.** 99

WHEN GREATER CONFIDENTIALITY WORKS BEST

An independent college with a strong tradition of shared governance was faced with hiring a new president for the first time in 12 years. Earlier searches had always included open campus visits by finalists so that constituents could meet and talk with the candidates and provide feedback to the search committee on their impressions. The college had improved significantly during the retiring president's tenure, so this search attracted an uncommonly talented pool of applicants, including a number of sitting college presidents. Most of these presidents

said they would need to withdraw from the search if forced to go through a public final step.

The board chair held open meetings on campus to describe an alternative, less open final step in the search, explaining that the college did not want to lose this promising segment of the candidate pool. Through extensive communication and open discussion, the college family agreed to a more closed process that was understood to be in the best interests of their institution.

contract. Campus visits offer the opportunity to assess other, more subtle, qualities in candidates. Can the candidate "work the room"? Is he or she comfortable in social situations? Can he or she speak comfortably to a nonacademic audience?

CAMPUS VISITS

Responsibility for planning the finalists' campus visits rests with the search committee. Because of the number of logistical details to be managed, it may set up a subcommittee to orchestrate the visits. If a group is already charged with transition planning, the search committee should involve it in its work at this time so that the search can lead seamlessly from campus visit through appointment to a well-thought-through and well-supported launch. If no such committee exists, this is an excellent time for the board to create one or otherwise ensure an effective transition is a central concern going forward.

Logistics

Finalist visits can be completed within two weeks if two days are allotted to each visit. This amount of time allows both candidates and campus ample opportunity to take each other's measure and leaves a small number of days for last-minute adjustments, transitions, and necessary rest. As with the neutral site interviews, visits should occur consecutively. Candidates should be spared the awkwardness of encountering one another. For fairness and purposes of comparison, each candidate should be asked to complete essentially the same set of activities.

The search committee chair should frame the campus visits for the community at this time. On the search's public website, the chair should: 1) review the process followed in selecting the finalists, acknowledging the benefit of stakeholders' input, 2) indicate the committee's great anticipation of their upcoming visits, and 3) explain the schedule. The chair may also need to explain the reasons certain groups and individuals have been chosen to meet with the candidates and to remind the community that while input from all will be important, the final decision and appointment will be the board's to make. The search committee chair will also want to set expectations for a hospitable reception, making the point that as the candidates cannot be assumed to have made up their minds, members of the campus community can be helpful by making them feel welcome. As part of this communication, identically formatted biographical summaries of the candidates should be provided.

Various search committee members can assume different roles during a candidate's visit. But each candidate should have one committee member or one administrative officer as host. The host should meet the candidate at the airport or wherever he or she arrives, make certain that overnight accommodations are satisfactory and attractive, guide the candidate from one appointment to another, make sure he or she arrives on time, and in general stay with the candidate until departure. The host's job is to introduce and to explain, make special arrangements when necessary, alter the schedule if desired, and answer questions the candidate might have about specific meetings. At group meetings, the host may be present to mediate if necessary, observe reactions, and interpret to the candidate afterwards why certain questions were raised and who pursued a certain line of inquiry. At individual conferences with administrative officers, the host's presence usually is not necessary and may interfere with candid communication.

Engaging Constituencies

A challenge for those planning the visits is finding ways to engage all appropriate constituencies in meaningful dialogue with each candidate within the time afforded by the visit. One state university scheduled campus visits over one and one-half days to include conversations and an open forum with board members, deans, cabinet-level administrators, faculty leaders, student government representatives, and alumni association leaders. The visit also included a dinner with board members and an exit debriefing with search committee members.

There are, of course, myriad ways to plan a campus visit, and no one way is superior to all others. But they almost always touch certain bases:

1. *Search committee:* The search committee generally has at least one substantial meeting with each candidate while he or she is on campus. Some committees find an initial meeting to be a useful and gracious introduction to the campus. Others prefer to end the visit with such a meeting to find out what kind of experience the candidate has had, what reactions and questions were generated, and what problems remain to be settled.

2. ***Board:*** A meeting or meetings with board members—or as many as can be available—is a near constant. These meetings may take the form of a structured conversation or a reception or informal social occasion, including a meal, or both. Conversations with the search committee chair and the board chair, separately or together, will almost invariably figure prominently on the schedule. Board leadership should make every effort to have as many board members as possible interact with each visiting finalist. The selection of one will be the single most important decision they make, and the full board must fully own it and embrace it with enthusiasm.

3. ***Departing president:*** Depending on the circumstances described earlier (*see Chapter 3, pages 23–25*), it might be desirable to have finalists meet with the departing president. This conversation can provide a helpful introduction to a potential mentor and give them important perspectives on the institution. Although the incumbent generally will not have a vote in the selection, his or her assessment of each finalist may be especially helpful.

4. ***Senior administrators:*** Although a case is often made for not including senior administrators on the search committee—if they would be put in the position of helping select their own future supervisor—they should now have direct access to each finalist and vice versa. These kinds of exchanges may best be facilitated by a series of conversations with one, two, or three senior staff members at a time. A sensible allotment of time—even time for a one-on-one conversation—will give more to those with the most authority and responsibility for revenues. Functional areas and titles vary, but on some campuses, for example, these participants might include the chief administrative officer, the chief financial officer, and the vice presidents for academic affairs, advancement, and enrollment management. Depending on the size and complexity of an institution, those planning the campus visits also may want to arrange individual conversations or small- or large-group meetings with a larger set of administrative staff. Those not specifically provided for in this way can be given opportunities to hear or meet the candidates in other settings. *(See "Other Constituents" below.)*

5. *Faculty:* At the very least, most visits will provide for a meeting with key faculty leaders, who may include deans, department chairs, faculty senate leaders, faculty union leaders, and the like. Or candidates may meet with the faculty as a whole. If so, candidates might be asked to prepare some remarks on a general topic or answer some standard questions that enable this audience to assess the candidate for itself, getting a sense of the candidate's values and how he or she thinks, speaks, and handles impromptu questioning.

6. *Other constituents:* With other constituencies—non-administrative staff, students, alumni, local officials, the local community, or representatives of the state education system—a few questions guide involvement:

   - Will there be one or more individual conversations?
   - Will there be a conversation with a small group selected to represent the larger constituency?
   - Will there be an effort to bring the candidate to an event to which the entire constituency has been invited?
   - Will it work to have several such gatherings over the course of the visit—for example, with students, faculty, and staff?
   - Or will it be better to invite everyone to an open forum where they have a chance to hear and possibly briefly meet the candidate?

Forums can provide a degree of access to several constituencies at once. Meals, receptions, even coffees and after-dinner drinks may work as well as, or better than, more structured events to satisfy demand for time with a candidate and foster good conversations. Whatever the final decisions, invitations must be extended, rooms reserved, local transportation arranged, and, generally, the days planned in full detail.

Of course, the candidates' capacity for undertaking the demanding work involved in campus visits must be considered. These visits are unavoidably strenuous, with much to be covered in a limited time. For those doing the search, however, setting up a fairly crowded and taxing schedule provides a great benefit. The new president will be living his or her professional life amid constant demands; it cannot hurt to observe each candidate under pressure.

SPOUSES, PARTNERS, AND FAMILIES

Given the changing nature of the work force, a growing number of presidents are women and many couples include two successful career professionals. For this reason, boards and search committees should be prepared to consider various alternatives, both for the possible role of an appointees' spouse or partner and for the participation of candidates' spouses and partners in the campus visit. Some presidents' spouses or partners will expect and welcome the traditional role—hosting events, particularly in the president's house, helping to entertain important friends and visitors, and the like. Some may have professional or academic credentials and seek full- or part-time employment as faculty, administrators, or development professionals. Others may prefer only limited involvement in campus activities. Thoughtful, sensitive discussions about expectations related to a potential president's spouse or partner need to begin before the candidate's campus visit. For its part, the board needs to reflect on past traditions and be prepared to consider different scenarios. Likewise, the candidate should be forthcoming about a spouse or partner's personal and professional expectations. *(See also "Spouse or Partner Compensation," Chapter 13.)*

Whatever roles spouses and partners may wish to assume, they are usually included in campus visits. More than ever, the decision to accept an offered presidency is a shared decision by the candidate and his or her spouse or partner. It can hinge on whether a new professional opportunity is attractive enough to warrant picking up roots, leaving jobs, children's schools, and social relationships behind in order to take it. These interested parties will want to know as much as possible about the potential new environment. It is very much in the institution's interest to welcome them, inform them, and do what it can to see that they feel positively disposed toward it.

The institution has an additional reason for wanting to include family members.

> **More than ever, accepting an offered presidency is a shared decision by the candidate and spouse or partner. It can hinge on whether a new professional opportunity is attractive enough to warrant picking up roots, leaving jobs, children's schools, and social relationships behind to take it.**

The visits are opportunities to meet individuals who might become important members of the campus community and inevitably, to one extent or another, represent the college. Learning about a spouse's or partner's interests and strengths, moreover, will prove particularly helpful if a role will be carved out in which he or she will be involved with the institution.

Attention to the needs and interests of candidates' families should begin well before the visit, with materials or emailed links that will enable them to learn about the campus and its immediate environs as well as the surrounding area. This information will give them a basis for deciding what they most want to explore when visiting, and arrangements can be tailored to their expressed needs and interests. The spouse or partner may want to know about employment opportunities in the community or on campus. If a couple has young children, both parents will be curious about schools and child care. A spouse or partner who runs marathons, plays string quartets, or volunteers may want to know about local opportunities.

Some of a spouse's or partner's agenda will overlap with that of the candidate. Typically, he or she would accompany the candidate to any social gatherings with board members or any large open forum. Since the candidate will be fully occupied in learning about the college or university, the spouse or partner may wish to schedule an independent visit with local school officials. If the campus offers a president's house, both will want to inspect it together, but if other housing arrangements are needed, a brief survey of local real estate may be appreciated. Every effort should be made to plan a constructive schedule.

Just as the candidate should have a host, so should the spouse, partner, or other family members who accompany him or her to campus. A particularly good choice would be someone who can stay involved as a special contact and resource throughout the transition period in the event that the candidate is appointed.

WRAPPING UP CAMPUS VISITS

All of these meetings with board and search committee members may need to focus not so much on discriminating among candidates as on making all candidates feel the institution could be a wonderful home. The visit should help each understand and appreciate the exciting opportunity the presidency presents. Campus visits are also final opportunities to ensure that important information has been disclosed and that candidates have had ample opportunity to ask questions.

First, keep in mind that nearly one in five presidents surveyed in the American Council on Education's study indicated he or she did not receive a full and accurate account of the institution's financial condition, and one in five reported not clearly understanding what would be expected of a president's spouse or partner.[27] Because omissions like these can seriously complicate a new presidency—or even enable a bad match of candidate and institution at the outset—boards and search committees will want to be scrupulous in their disclosures to anyone who might subsequently receive an offer.

Second, if the terms of employment are not discussed until time of appointment, the committee and the board risk the withdrawal of the chosen candidate, who may find the terms unacceptable. If they delay until a public announcement has been made, they are even more vulnerable. Negotiation of salary and perquisites is not the proper function of a search committee but of the board. In practice, the executive or compensation committee handles the negotiations and brings a final recommendation to the full board for review and approval. So the search committee chair or board chair should take the initiative during their conversations with each candidate to update him or her as to what the college or university is prepared to offer—not necessarily the precise terms but certainly the range of total compensation.

Third, the end of the visit is the time to find out whether, in light of all he or she has learned, the candidate is still actively interested. After a long day of meetings, receptions, and dinner with the board, the chair of the board or search committee often has a private conversation with the candidate. After observing very positive signals about the candidate's reception on campus, the chair may tell the candidate that he or she is one of three or four finalists whom the committee is prepared to recommend to the board and that the committee needs to know: "Will you accept the position, if offered, assuming that satisfactory terms can be negotiated?" An unequivocal answer should be sought.

Some candidates object to this question because the decision is too complex and

---

[27] *American College President* 2012, p. 46.

too momentous to be made unless they are dealing with an actual offer. One can sympathize with this reaction. At the same time, the offer of the presidency is a complex and momentous decision for the board. If an offer is made, word sometimes leaks out. If the offer is turned down, the resulting situation may be awkward. Other candidates, who under other circumstances would be happy to accept, may withdraw their names. To protect the reputation of the candidates as well as their own self-interests, board members need to know in advance whether a candidate is likely to accept the offer, assuming a mutually agreeable contract can be negotiated.

EVALUATING THE FINALISTS AND MAKING A RECOMMENDATION

While it is the search committee's responsibility to evaluate the finalists and the board's to select one to be president, the thoughts and reactions of all those who have seen and interacted with the candidates should be actively sought out. Online survey instruments are easily created and accessed and provide instant tabulation of results. The questions asked should reflect the criteria set out in the position profile, and there should be a place for open-ended comments. To inhibit interest-group politics, the search committee should inform all would-be respondents that only individuals are permitted to assess the candidates. And to encourage the evaluation of each candidate on his or her own merits rather than on comparisons with others, the comment period on each candidate should close before the next candidate's appearance on campus.

As soon as possible after the last candidate leaves campus, the search committee should reconvene. This meeting, four to five months into the search for a new president, will be the committee's seventh or eighth (not counting its conversations with individual candidates during their campus visits), and it usually will be its final meeting overall. After completing any additional reference calls made during or immediately after the campus visits, the committee ideally will have before it all the evidence needed to execute its charge: the recommendation of candidates to the board. In addition to the candidates' letters of application and CVs, the committee will have the results of numerous reference calls, a deep background check, all that has been learned from neutral-site interviews and two-day visits, and the advice and counsel of those in the community who responded to the post-visit surveys. The committee's information may be particularly current and nuanced if the search firm has been discreetly at work on the committee's behalf, finding out still more about the candidates, communicating with them to: monitor their participation in other searches, assess their levels of interest, answer their concerns, and "keep them warm."

The committee must now make its own evaluations and forward them to the board in accordance with the details of its charge. The charge may specify one of three options:

SEARCHES IN STATE UNIVERSITY SYSTEMS

Most observations and prescriptions in this book apply to searches for the chief executive of a state system. But these searches differ in some key ways.

A primary fact of life in many system searches is the need to conduct business openly, to one degree or another, due to state sunshine laws. (*See "Special Issues for Public Institutions," Chapter 6.*) A state system search will be designed to comply with these strictures, but, in reality, also to preserve whatever confidentiality can be achieved under the law.

System search committees typically include board of regents members, a few system campus presidents, state system staff, and others. It is important that a reasonably broad sample of campuses be represented, as this gives candidates a view of the system's diversity and allows the campuses a more significant voice in the deliberations.

The use of search firms is universal. The firm, in consultation with the search committee,

develops the position profile for board approval. It also takes the lead in advertising, seeking nominations, and recruiting.

Searches in state systems pay special attention to attracting candidates from within the system and from other state systems, including executive officers, other senior administrators, and campus presidents. Other sources of candidates might include government officials, military leaders, and business leaders, but a primary qualification will usually be an understanding of how a system works. The search committee screens candidates and selects a short list. As due diligence is conducted, the committee schedules and hosts preliminary interviews.

A list of finalists is developed after the preliminary interviews and forwarded to the board of regents, which hosts the final interviews. The board also completes the due diligence and extends the offer to the favored candidate.

1. **One candidate's name** is to be forwarded as the committee's *recommended choice.*
2. **A specific number** (or up to a number, or a range of numbers) of names are to be forwarded, *in ranked order.*
3. **Several candidates** are to be forwarded, *unranked.*

The third option is probably the best course, for the reasons explained in Chapter 5. The flexibility afforded by several choices can prove the difference between a failed search and a successful one, as preferred candidates sometimes withdraw, typically to accept other offers or because they find the terms of a final offer unsatisfactory. As for ranking, the comments that the committee provides on each candidate can make its relative judgments quite clear without tying the board's hands. An unranked list will help prevent a situation in which the board's independent review might lead it to "overturn the search committee's decision."

Once the search committee has deliberated, arrived at its conclusions, and reported to the board, its major assignment is complete. The committee chair may communicate the report to the board chair. But some chairs—or even their entire boards—may want to meet with the search committee to discuss its recommendations. Boards also want varying amounts of information on each candidate and the committee's processes. Some committee members, of course, may continue to participate in the selection as board members. And some may—and should—help to ensure a successful post-appointment transition.

A few tasks remain at this point. Unsuccessful candidates must be thanked and notified that they are not moving forward. Announcements must be prepared. *(See "Announcing the Appointment," Chapter 13, pages 139–141.)* Committee records should be prepared and filed for future reference, and electronic and paper files should be organized and secured. (A search firm generally will retain its records on all candidates for one year.) Apart from these and some other responsibilities for wrap-up and transition, the final steps belong to the board, which must make the appointment and set the terms and conditions.

Key Points

- **Open campus visits benefit both the candidates and the campus community** because each has an opportunity to see and interact with the other firsthand.

- **Engage all important constituencies in dialogue with the candidates** as time allows. Arrange for private conversations with the search committee, its chair, and other board members, including the board chair.

- **Focus on the needs and interests of the candidates' spouses, partners, and families**, who will want to know as much as possible about the campus and the community.

- **Evaluate the finalists in light of all that has been learned** and, in accordance with the search committee's charge, make recommendations to the board. Naming several candidates without ranking them offers the board the greatest flexibility.

Additional Article from *Trusteeship*

Bacow, Lawrence S. and Adele Fleet Bacow, "The Changing Roles of Presidential Spouses." *Trusteeship* (March/April 2008): p. 40.

Horner, David and David A. Williams, "Does the Presidential Spouse Have a Role? Should the Role Be Compensated?" *Trusteeship* (March/April 2013): pp. 22–25.

For more recommended reading, please see Resources at the end of this book.

Part

IV | MOVING FORWARD: PRESIDENTIAL SELECTION AND TRANSITION

Chapter 13

Selecting and Appointing a New President

"The board needs to realize that the end game is now at hand."

AFTER THE SEARCH COMMITTEE gives the board its recommendations, the board takes over full responsibility for the search's concluding steps. These tasks include any additional vetting required, selecting the candidate to whom it wishes to extend an offer (and possibly one or two alternates, in rank order), and setting the terms of appointment.

MAKING A CHOICE AND EXTENDING AN OFFER

Because it is the board's responsibility alone to select a president, its review of the candidates must be fresh and independent. So if the board chair, search committee chair, or search consultant thinks that the board will need or want additional information or a different perspective on a candidate, they certainly can be in touch with anyone they choose. In some cases, one or two leading finalists may need to be brought back for a quick series of conversations, particularly if a few board members have had no opportunity to meet them.

At this stage, though, time constraints come more and more into play. The clock ticks audibly. A candidate's enthusiasm for and confidence about a new professional opportunity can fade quickly as other searches produce offers, home institutions produce counter-offers, or candidates mull over what they now know. In these final hours, the best-positioned boards will have worked with their search committees to ensure due diligence, considered the terms of appointment carefully, and remained in steady contact with the most competitive candidates about these terms and the candidates' intentions to accept them, if offered. The board needs to realize that the end game is now at hand. It requires a conscious push to make a selection and an offer with dispatch and to react nimbly to any of the most likely scenarios.

As mentioned in Chapter 12, as soon as possible after the campus visits, the full board meets. Here the board, with the help of the search consultant, reviews the search committee's recommendations and results of any additional research, reference calls, or conversations with candidates. It selects one finalist to receive an offer and possibly chooses one or two alternates.

The board authorizes the board chair, search committee chair, or an executive committee member to call the candidate to extend the offer, and it will, in one of several ways, approve the terms of the appointment—the framework of conditions and circumstances of employment. The board should confirm the final terms if they have already been negotiated, set final terms itself, or vote authority to the chair to settle the final terms within appropriate parameters. Logistically, giving the chair such authority is clearly preferable.

At some public institutions, state sunshine laws mandate an open meeting to vote on the new president. This meeting's agenda will be more limited. *(See "Compliance," pages 54–55 and "Special Issues for Public Institutions," pages 60–61 in Chapter 6; and sidebar, page 122.)*

Most candidates, upon receiving an offer, need some time to consult family, friends, and colleagues. But the board should not hesitate to ask for a quick response, perhaps within two working days. This request is especially warranted when care has been taken to inform finalists of the likely terms in advance and when they, in turn, have said they are likely to accept. Candidates also need to take realistic account of the institution's situation.

Candidates can accept the offer in its original form, ask for time to consider the offer, propose a counter-offer, or propose language and compensation different from that in the board's offer. At times, the candidate and the board retain professionals to represent them in contract negotiations, or both ask a neutral third party to facilitate their conversations. Regardless of the process, contract negotiations can be contentious and will require steady, mature, and confident planning and communication.

If the candidate with an offer declines it, the board faces a doubly unappealing prospect. It suffers not only the loss of its first choice, but also the passage of more time waiting for a decision from another candidate. Meanwhile, that candidate too has had to wait and wonder and has perhaps fallen prey to second thoughts. If a second candidate declines, the situation only worsens. The longer the process takes, the more difficult it becomes to preserve confidentiality and the more likely rumors are to spread, complicating and possibly undercutting the entire search effort.

A WRITTEN CONTRACT

Fortunately, a search that has proceeded with due attention to planning and communication has a very good chance of seeing its first offer accepted—and, if not the first, then the second. Understandably, those involved feel excitement and satisfaction at the moment an offer is accepted. This signals the impending culmination of a long, at times arduous, process and the search's likely success in renewing the institution's top leadership. Yet in most cases acceptance does not complete the task of securing a new president. A contract usually needs to be finalized. This step is significant. A board and a candidate who has accepted sometimes do fail to reach agreement on specifics, and the candidate withdraws or is dropped from consideration.

The agreement between the board and the new president should be recorded in a formal, written document that systematically outlines, at a minimum, duties, terms of service, direct and indirect compensation, arrangements for performance assessment, review of compensation, and termination criteria. Putting a written contract in place is more than tying up loose ends. It is a way of forcing healthy, necessary conversations at the right moment between the board and the president-elect about expectations, needs, working styles, communication, evaluation, and other matters that are the foundation of a successful presidency. The old-school notion that "my word is my bond" is being increasingly overtaken by the reality that "if it's not in writing, it never happened." In any case, as of 2011 more than three in four serving presidents had received written contracts with their job offers.[28] Here best practice and common practice converge. The difference between a contract and a contractual letter is a fine one, but the difference between a written and an oral agreement is the difference between a good operation and a sloppy one.

With the ascendance of written employment contracts, both institutions and presidential finalists are more likely to seek advice from third parties. A board chair can rely on the search consultant and the institution's general counsel or outside attorney, if not one or more lawyers specializing in tax and employment contracts. Recourse to outside expertise—if not outright delegation of negotiating responsibilities—is often quite appropriate. Recent research indicates that more than 44 percent of current presidents have also sought negotiating advice at the time of their appointments from family members, colleagues in the field, and attorneys.[29]

Clearly, getting the details right is important to both sides. To achieve that, negotiations sometimes produce elaborate documents that detail agreements about all aspects of the employment relationship. But contracts need not be exhaustively long and difficult.

The board should not only approve the terms of appointment in a contract—at least as presented to it in general terms—but it should also have access to the final product. The contract need not be handed out in an open meeting. The compensation committee, executive committee, or other appropriate group or person should make it available on request under controlled circumstances. For most, a report from the chair will be sufficient.

LENGTH OF TERM AND PLANS FOR SEPARATION

The length of the term of employment usually reflects some compromise between the individual's need to have a period of commitment and the institution's need to review performance and possibly make adjustments within a reasonable time. The sweet spot is often three years. Only a small minority of candidates—and very few stronger ones—will happily accept a one-year term. A five-year term is not uncommon, although it is sometimes seen as risky if the contract requires the payout of benefits over that long a

---

[28] Ibid.

[29] Ibid.

term in the event of a separation. These three term lengths—one, three, and five or more years—are used in 18 percent, 37 percent, and 29 percent, respectively, of presidential contracts today.[30] In some states the issue is moot, as they permit no terms, only service at the pleasure of the board.

> **❝ The length of the term of employment reflects compromise between the new president's need for commitment and the institution's need to review performance and possibly make adjustments...The sweet spot is often three years." ❞**

A president's eventual departure may result from an agreed-upon schedule; board dissatisfaction with the president's performance or the president's with the board's; retirement, disability, or death; interest in an outside opportunity; or some combination of these reasons. A wise board will anticipate each possible type of separation in its contract. The board needs to know, for example, that the new president will not desert on short notice, and the president needs assurance that he or she will be given, say, reasonable leave with salary if circumstances require a change. Further, the absence of clear termination arrangements can lead to expensive and damaging lawsuits. Both at the outset of the first period of service and as contracts are renewed, the terms, conditions, and circumstances of separation should be specified.

Termination without cause, from the board's point of view, is often the cleanest basis for separation from employment, allowing the removal of a problematic incumbent without the details having to be made public. At the same time, it may entail a negotiated severance package, and it can encourage abrupt departures. The following questions should be considered:

- Will either party be able to end the relationship without showing cause within, say, 30 days?
- Will there be a provision for severance pay in the event a president is removed? If so, for how long?
- Will a termination agreement include a release of any claims the president has against the institution?

When a president with appropriate academic credentials steps down on more or less

---

[30] Ibid., p. 97.

amicable terms, other questions must be asked:

- Will he or she be able to assume a faculty position?
- If so, what will be the understanding regarding rank and tenure?
- Should he or she be given a transition sabbatical of six months to a year with no duties other than getting up to speed again in the academic field?
- If so, will travel and living expenses be covered? (This is a common benefit, partly because it encourages the individual to leave campus following the end of the appointment.)

PROVIDING FOR PERFORMANCE ASSESSMENT

The periodic assessment of a president's leadership is one of the board's most basic responsibilities. It should include both annual evaluations and comprehensive reviews every four or five years. Together these two forms of assessment "help draw out the strengths and the best possibilities of the president in achieving both short and long-term goals," according to Richard L. Morrill in *Assessing Presidential Effectiveness* (AGB Press, 2010). Benefits include:

- For the president and the board, a clear sense of the president's past and current performance measured against goals;
- For the board, the opportunities they need to assess the president's readiness for future challenges;
- Occasions for candid and mutually supportive exchange and chances to address together minor or emerging problems before they become more serious; and
- The basis for appropriate periodic adjustments in presidential salary and benefits.

Any college or university board—and any new president—will want an effective system of regular performance appraisal to be mandated in the employment contract. Eighty-seven percent of presidents in 2011 had contracts that call for annual performance evaluations conducted by boards or board subcommittees (60 percent), system heads (20 percent), or board chairs (14 percent).[31] Comparable figures are not available on the frequency and

---

[31] Ibid., p. 98.

nature of the comprehensive evaluations conducted every four or five years. But these assessments are especially critical to the board's understanding of the president's ability to lead going forward, given the particular challenges his or her institution faces. Although the contract is not the place to spell out the details of a performance evaluation system, it should support and be fully consistent with documents elsewhere that do. [32]

SETTING COMPENSATION

Most boards recognize that the modern academic presidency is an all-consuming commitment, and compensation levels must be competitive in order for colleges and universities to attract and retain visionary chief executives capable of leading them. In recent years, however, issues surrounding executive compensation have become increasingly challenging for governing boards. Corporate scandals led in 2002 to passage of the Sarbanes-Oxley Act, a touchstone for many college and university board members who work in the corporate sector. Executive compensation figured in a series of highly publicized governance failures in the nonprofit sector, prompting congressional leaders to call for greater oversight of nonprofit boards. Attention from the Internal Revenue Service has intensified the spotlight on the conduct of their fiduciary responsibilities. And a vigorous, ongoing debate in the higher education press concerning presidential compensation is part of the larger societal discussion about CEO pay in general. In this environment, boards must be vigilant as they set compensation levels and willing and prepared to publicly defend those levels as fair and appropriate.

This section sets out key considerations regarding compensation in higher education. In addition to availing themselves of this guidance, boards and search committees should seek the assistance early on of professionals who specialize in presidential compensation. [33] The Resources section at the end of this book suggests further reading on compensation in higher education.

---

[32] A particularly useful source on best practice relating to presidential performance evaluation is Richard L. Morrill, *Assessing Presidential Effectiveness: A Guide for College and University Boards* (Washington, DC: AGB, 2010).

[33] See especially Robert Atwell, *Presidential Compensation in Higher Education: A Guide for Governing Boards* (Washington, DC: AGB, 2008).

Federal Law

The two most pertinent areas of federal law are the IRS intermediate sanctions requirements and the Form 990 disclosures. Both apply only to section 501(c)(3) organizations, but these groups include public college and university foundations. As a result, if a public institution's foundation or other private source supplements presidential compensation—the case at about one in three such institutions—these laws and regulations are germane.[34]

Intermediate sanctions are tax penalties that the IRS can levy against the president and members of the governing board if the IRS finds evidence of "excess benefits" in salary and benefit practices—that is, pay and benefits that appear too high for the market, in the judgment of the IRS, or that raise questions about the nonprofit organization's purposes. But intermediate sanctions essentially address the policies and procedures for setting and reviewing presidential compensation rather than the actual salary or benefit levels. Boards must therefore be careful to follow and document procedures that create what the IRS terms a "rebuttable presumption" that salaries and benefits represent fair-market compensation. Examples of indicators that help assure the IRS that the board's compensation decisions are appropriate include:

- *No financial interest:* Evidence that the decisions are made by a delegated subset of board members, typically the executive committee or a separate compensation committee, who have no financial interest in the decision;
- *Comparative data:* Documentation that compensation is generally appropriate to the market and is set using data from institutions that would generally be considered comparable; and
- *Performance reviews:* Evidence that compensation decisions follow the board's review of presidential performance.

The privileges of enjoying financial support through direct appropriation and tax-exempt status come at a cost to colleges and universities. They are required to disclose to the public a variety of information. While most states allow personnel discussions

---

[34] Nancy L. Zimpher, "Presidential Turnover and the Institutional Community: Restarting and Moving Forward," in Martin and Samels, *Presidential Transition*, pp. 116–117.

and a few other matters to be held in executive session, some require that these discussions be conducted in public or that the results be reported in public session. As a result, the salaries of most public college and university presidents, and sometimes the full details of their compensation packages, are matters of public record. Although independent institutions hold these topics closer to the vest, the Form 990 disclosure requirements are changing this reality. The form—similar to the 10K, 10Q, and proxy information filed by corporations—solicits, among other things, the names and salaries of the chief executive and other senior executives; the names of all directors (board members) and what if anything they are paid; whether the latter conduct any business with the institution; and basic revenues, expenditures, and net assets. All independent colleges and universities must make copies of their Form 990s available to individuals upon request.

Data from Comparable Institutions

One set of necessary reference points for determining an appropriate level of compensation is established by information obtained from other colleges and universities. National surveys miss many institutions, provide limited disaggregation, and underreport information about benefits, deferred compensation, and supplements from university foundations. As a result, they are unlikely to provide the data needed. Intermediate sanction regulations strongly suggest a focus on peer institutions, those that would generally be considered closely comparable in terms of control (public or independent, for-profit or not), enrollment, endowment, and other such variables. Other factors will also affect decisions on the compensation level, including the candidate's current salary, the compensation of the institution's senior administrators and faculty, and the history and culture of the institution.

Smaller institutions can generally do an adequate job of researching comparable institutions on their own. If a group of peers—which should be actual rather than aspirational—is identified and surveyed, response rates can usually be boosted by promising to share the resulting data. But for comparable data on presidential compensation at larger, more complex institutions, a compensation consultant may well be needed. Their firms are often called upon for the heavy lifting involved in setting external benchmarks—collecting, aggregating, and contextualizing reliable data—and they often maintain proprietary databases for this purpose.

Elements of the Compensation Package

Salary, benefits, and retirement and deferred compensation are basic elements of the compensation package. Various perquisites also may be included. As of 2011, aside from base salary the following were the most common conditions of employment:

- Pension/retirement contributions *(in 85 percent of contracts)*;
- Life insurance *(70 percent)*;
- Automobile, with or without driver *(69 percent)*;
- Merit-based salary increases *(45 percent)*;
- Club memberships *(42 percent)*;
- Professional development *(40 percent)*;
- Entertainment *(40 percent)*;
- President's house *(37 percent)*;
- Deferred compensation *(36 percent)*; and
- Provisions for health and wellness *(33 percent)*.

The average contract contained substantially more elements in 2011 than in 2006, the last year all institutions were surveyed. Some conditions of employment—like performance or time-based bonuses, sabbaticals, and license to serve as a paid member of a corporate board—became markedly more common over that same period.[35]

Annual Compensation: Salary and Bonus

The contract should state the initial salary along with the process for considering future increases. Ordinarily it will indicate that the president is eligible for all benefits provided to other senior administrators, then spell out any additional compensation and benefits to be received.

Ten years ago, performance bonuses were rarely a part of presidential compensa-

---

[35] *American College President* 2012, p. 98.

tion, but now they are increasingly common. Advocates make the case that if presidential bonuses can provide the incentive to achieve critical institutional goals, they are entirely appropriate. Boards using them should be clear as to the specific metrics. The trigger might be a certain percentage increase in endowment or enrollment, for example, and the bonus a certain percentage of the base salary. Bonuses, of course, do not augment the salary base for future years (an attractive cost-control feature), and they are taxable upon receipt.

At many public institutions, presidential compensation is supplemented from the resources of college- or university-affiliated foundations. These supplements should be made according to spelled-out policies and procedures and publicly disclosed. Again, since such foundations are 501(c)(3) organizations, these kinds of payments are subject to IRS scrutiny.

Retirement and Deferred Compensation

Boards should be aware that federal law limits the extent to which they may augment presidential compensation through enhanced benefits or retirement packages. It prohibits, for example, "tax-qualified" retirement benefits substantially greater than those paid to other employees. Limitations also differ according to institutional control (public vs. independent). Here, too, seeking outside expertise may be in order.

Partly because of the limitations mentioned, deferred compensation has become a common way for boards to enhance presidential compensation packages. Options are more limited than in the corporate sector and include qualified governmental "excess benefit plans," Section 457 deferred compensation plans, and Section 403(b) tax-sheltered annuities. Secular trusts, group life insurance plans, annuities, bonus life insurance plans, and split-dollar insurance plans each may have features that recommend them in particular cases. Given the frequent complexity of these and similar instruments, their current tax implications, and the evolution of tax laws themselves, boards are encouraged to approach the shaping of a deferred compensation package only with expert assistance.

Spouse or Partner Compensation

A final form of financial compensation to be dealt with in many cases is payment to the president's spouse or partner. These individuals typically put in long hours "meeting and greeting" at campus events, planning and assisting with fundraising efforts, and attending off-campus gatherings. Boards should discuss these matters fully with spouses and partners of newly selected presidents and not be presumptuous in expecting them to carry out social and other responsibilities. *(See also Chapter 12, Spouses, Partners, and Families.)*

According to the most recent ACE study of all presidents, 14 percent of spouses or partners are employed or compensated by their partners' institutions. Other recent studies suggest the practice is much more common at smaller and private institutions. Boards may certainly compensate those who do work and wish to be paid.[36] At the same time, if the spouse or partner is to be paid, he or she should be treated like other employees. His or her salary must be justified by supervised performance of a carefully drawn job description. The IRS may well evaluate whatever compensation is provided to determine whether it is at market rates.

The board should know, nonetheless, that negotiations regarding compensation for a new president's spouse or partner are a perennial minefield. Frequently viewed as a form of nepotism, such remuneration can generate vocal opposition from many quarters, including faculty, staff, local media, and some board members. Spouses who do not take compensated employment may still, of course, perform significant institutional roles. And boards should consider all their options for assisting and recognizing a spouse's or partner's contributions. For example, the college or university could provide event-planning assistance for the latter's efforts related to fundraising, campus celebrations, and alumni activities. The board can also recognize the spouse as an employee for purposes of business travel so that he or she can be covered by university insurance.

---

[36] *American College President* 2012, p. 47; Raymond D. Cotton, "Paying the President's Spouse," *Chronicle of Higher Education*, May 23, 2003; and David G. Horner and S. Sue Horner, "The Role of the Presidential Spouse/Partner," *University Business*, January 15, 2013.

Other Benefits

Among the remaining elements often covered in the employment contract, housing warrants especially careful attention. Many institutions provide either a house or a housing allowance to the president. If living in the house is a condition of employment and the house is on or very near the campus (like the apartment above the store), then the value of the house or housing subsidy is not considered a taxable benefit. The employment agreement should therefore state that the president is required to reside in the house. Many go beyond that to state that, should the IRS classify as taxable income all or part of the compensation related to housing, the institution will increase the salary by the amount necessary to pay the additional tax. If the housing in question is off campus, it is especially important to maintain records documenting that it is used in a significant and continuous fashion.

A complete contract might enumerate a host of other benefits, including: reimbursement for automobile expenses; relocation and moving expenses; tuition remission for dependents; travel, communication, entertainment, and related expenses; child care; long-term care insurance; and outside financial and legal counsel.

The contract will typically spell out expectations regarding academic rank and tenure status (which should be granted through normal academic channels, not unilaterally by the board) and whether the president will have membership on the institution's own governing board. (Most serve ex officio and have no vote.) Limitations on outside employment and opportunities for service on other boards, both corporate and nonprofit, may also be addressed.

ANNOUNCING THE APPOINTMENT

The choice has been made and the terms at last agreed upon. There remains the public announcement, which is an institutional responsibility, and the private notification to unsuccessful candidates, which is the search committee's task. Both have been anticipated in the communications plan drafted at the outset of the search. The two aspects now need to be coordinated.

Excitement will be high and rumors rampant. There is every reason for making a public announcement at the earliest possible point, with agreement by all parties on the precise timing. The president-elect must have the time to notify colleagues and superiors before they hear the news from other sources. But little can remain secret for long, and news—and rumor—is shared today almost instantaneously, so the appointee should make quick work of this. All involved should think in terms of hours, not days.

The search committee must also move very fast to notify any finalists who have not already bowed out of the picture. Telephone calls will be the most considerate way to inform them of the choice. No one who has any reason to believe he or she might still be in the running should learn of the decision from a media report, as has been the case in more instances than one would like to believe. Not only is prior notification the professional and decent thing, it also gives disappointed finalists far less reason to convey to others a bad image of the institution.

Unless state laws dictate otherwise, board and search committee members, as well as faculty, student, and administrative staff leaders, should be informed before the public announcement. So should a short list of influential friends, including large donors, influential legislators, and key corporate and foundation contacts.[37] The entire campus should then be apprised of the appointment. Depending on the size and character of the institution, this might be done in a specially called gathering or by special announcement through whatever media can best spread the word in timely fashion. The same website that chronicles the search effort should prominently feature the news. The new president should be given full discretion to decide whether it is more important to be on his or her new campus at the time of the announcement or on the one that will be absorbing the news of a probably unexpected departure.

Media kits will next need to be distributed. Copies of an announcement might be sent to all candidates and to those who have nominated candidates, with appropriate cover letters thanking them for their interest and help. A little extra effort at this point will only enhance the institution's reputation.

Alumni will need to be informed as soon as possible. A special email announcement or letter from the committee or the board chair might be considered, followed by an article in the alumni magazine reviewing the search, selection, and appointment. In

---

[37] Ross, "Leaks Kill," in Martin and Samels, *Presidential Transition*, p. 183.

the days and weeks that follow, good use should be made of all institutional publications, including magazines, websites, and newsletters reaching constituencies inside and outside the college or university.

As the appointing officer, the board chair typically announces the new president's selection. In doing so—as well as in presenting the president at events and through other written announcements—he or she will want to convey a set of key messages.

The announcement of the new president is an exciting time to look forward and to introduce new perspectives and new energy to the campus. Most institutions celebrate this moment as an occasion that brings the campus together and welcomes the new president. Jean A. Dowdall, who has led many leadership searches in higher education, offers these talking points for a presidential announcement:

- We are pleased that such a distinguished individual will be assuming the presidency.
- We will hold a number of events where everyone can meet him or her.
- We celebrate the excellent contributions of the previous president.
- We are enormously grateful to all those who participated in the search process.
- We thank those who have led the institution during any interim.
- We are already at work on planning the transition. A broadly representative group will help to ensure a warm welcome and the smooth launch of the new presidency.[38]

Key Points

- **After additional vetting, the board should meet to select the finalist to whom it wishes to make an offer** and possibly one or two others as alternates. It should approve at least the basic outline of that offer, possibly leaving the negotiation to the board chair, search consultant, or legal counsel.

- **Both the board and the candidate it chooses should move quickly** to bring the process to a close.

---

[38] Dowdall, *Searching for Higher Education Leadership*, pp. 151–52.

- **Prepare a written employment contract** that sets out the length of the initial term and provides a process for performance evaluation and renewal, as well as plans for possible separation. The contract should present a compensation package designed through a process consistent with federal law and regulations and include such elements as salary, benefits, and retirement and deferred compensation.

- **As the culmination of updates posted throughout the search, announce the new president's appointment** in a carefully coordinated series of communications to all interested constituencies.

Additional Articles from *Trusteeship*

Morrill, Richard L. "Assessing Presidential Effectiveness." *Trusteeship* (January/February 2010): p. 8.

MacTaggart, Terrence. "How Presidential Evaluations Must Change." *Trusteeship* (January/February 2012): p. 8.

Oden, Teresa Johnston. "Let's Talk About Paying the President's Spouse." *Trusteeship* (March/April 2005): pp. 29 – 32.

For more recommended reading, please see Resources at the end of this book.

Chapter 14

Launching a New Presidency

"To lead effectively, the president will need to come to understand an entire new campus community."

CONSIDER THE NEWLY APPOINTED college or university president: an able and experienced figure, with a strong claim on the good will of the institution, ready to go to work, and brimming with enthusiasm and ideas of what can be done to improve the place. In short, this person is a sight for sore board members' eyes—even more so considering the time, money, and hard work that have gone into the search.

But consider also what this welcome and reassuring figure faces. His or her job performance will be important and highly visible to many people—people who will not hesitate to pass judgment on it. The job requires, typically, meeting an array of stiff challenges in academic, financial, political, and other arenas. To lead effectively, the president will need to come to understand an entire new campus community. He or she will need to meet students, faculty, staff, board members, alumni, donors, and local citizens, impress them favorably, and hear their concerns. It will be critical to understand and analyze the institution and its options. Facts must be gathered and processes understood. Existing human, physical, and financial assets must be appraised. New networks of friends and allies will have to be created and new resources identified—and probably some agendas blunted or disarmed. The new president will need to win the community's confidence and, ideally, its enthusiastic support for his or her initiatives. Typically, the president must achieve all this—and a good number of early successes—within a short period, a year or less, perhaps even six months. Moreover, during this early period, the new appointee must tread carefully to avoid costly missteps.

In the excitement of the announcement, which often comes after a complex and demanding search process and perhaps after a contentious relationship with the previous president, it is important to remember that the board's obligations continue. As a former president of the University of California, Clark Kerr, put it, "the responsibility of the board for a new president does not end with a sigh of relief and a crossing of the fingers."[39] If only because of the difficulty of the new president's charge, boards should do all they possibly can to facilitate an appointee's transition into office, and they should set the stage in the early months of the presidency for effectiveness over the longer term. If more boards did so, fewer presidents would have reason to report, ruefully, having been dropped at the gate, and more presidencies would survive the critical early years to meet the prodigious expectations boards and others invest in them.

Studies of the process by which new executives take charge of their organizations identify the first three to six months as particularly critical.[40] This is the entry phase, when impressions are formed, important relationships are established, the learning curve is steepest, and too often irreparable mistakes are made. A full year or more may be required for the appointee to become immersed in the new institution and fully assume the reins of power, and presidents need to be supported throughout. But the first three to six months demand special attention.

STEPS THE BOARD SHOULD TAKE

The board is responsible for much of the most critical early work. The board's leadership should first ensure clarity of expectations. Immediately after the appointment, the board chair and the president should begin developing performance goals for the term allotted.

---

[39] Clark Kerr, quoted in Patricia Stanley and Lee J. Betts, "A Proactive Model for Presidential Transition," in Martin and Samels, *Presidential Transition*, p. 84.

[40] Don Tebbe, *Chief Executive Transitions: How to Hire and Support a Nonprofit CEO* (Washington, DC: BoardSource, 2008), p. 64.

Built squarely upon the needs outlined in the position profile, goals should be ambitious, achievable, and have the strong support of both parties. These goals, expressed in terms of agreed-to metrics, can provide the benchmarks for subsequent evaluation.

Just as important is clarifying expectations of other sorts that affect board-president relations. Many of these go to questions of communications and decision making:

- What budgetary authority does the president have?
- What decisions (on legal or personnel matters, for example) need board approval?
- What issues should be discussed with, say, the full board, the executive committee, the chair?
- How should the president communicate between board meetings?
- What information needs to be shared with the board, and how does the board prefer to have it presented?[41]

Less clear-cut but equally important is the matter of building mutual confidence—a process that should have a good foundation in the board's audit of its own effectiveness. *(See Chapter 7, page 70.)* The relationship of the chair and the president is all-important and well worth special attention. The two should make every effort to spend time together in ways that will foster trust and productivity. Programs such as AGB's Institute for Board Chairs and Presidents provide structured opportunities for these two key figures to shape a close, productive working relationship. Board members collectively need to demonstrate early in a presidency that they will be strong allies and partners. They can make helpful introductions, provide contacts, give of their own resources and assist in fundraising, attend important campus events, stand behind the president whenever possible in controversial matters, be candid about their concerns, and not press personal agendas. One or two particularly experienced board members may be able to assist informally as senior counselors and ambassadors in ways that those reporting to the new president or less well-connected in the community cannot.

---

[41] Susan Resneck Pierce, "Boards and Presidents—After the Hire," *Inside Higher Ed*, March 6, 2009, http://www.insidehighered.com/advice/2009/03/06/pierce.

An important way boards can support new presidents is by encouraging them to take advantage of opportunities to acquire skills and understanding they need to do their jobs effectively. Few successful candidates for presidencies spend time during searches calling attention to areas in which they are insufficiently prepared. But all new presidents have them. The 2011 ACE survey of presidents asked respondents whether they were sufficiently skilled in each of a long list of areas. These areas were most identified as weaknesses:

- Fundraising *(mentioned by 40 percent)*;
- Technology planning *(34 percent)*;
- Risk management/legal issues *(30 percent)*;
- Capital improvement projects *(27 percent)*;
- Entrepreneurial ventures *(27 percent)*; and
- Campus internationalization *(25 percent)*.

At least one in five cited deficiencies in these areas:

- Athletics *(24 percent)*;
- Budget/financial management *(24 percent)*;
- Government relations *(22 percent)*;
- Governing board relations *(22 percent)*; and
- Enrollment management *(20 percent)*.[42]

Relevant learning opportunities are available from established training programs for new presidents (for example, the Harvard Seminar for New Presidents) and the wide array of topical conferences offered by national higher education groups like ACE, the Council for Advancement and Support of Education (CASE), and the National Association of College and University Business Officers (NACUBO).

As search consultant Ted Marchese reminds us, small but effective ways can smooth a transition. It is wise not to overload a president-elect; he or she is likely trying to wrap up current responsibilities in a professional manner. Moreover, the appointee needs some time off before starting at a new institution. So, if possible, allow some time

---

[42] *American College President* 2012, p. 99.

for preparation, reflection, and recharging of energies. Another common-sense prescription is creating a presidential discretionary fund. It will be appreciated as critical marginal support for work on new initiatives. It creates a means for a president to signal what he or she values and can generate early forward movement.[43] This last objective is often served by the new president's coming to campus for focused periods before assuming duties. Meetings at these times with key people and groups can help a president hit the ground running on day one.

Board members should be alert—more in this early period than at any other time—to the possibility of major presidential missteps, however innocent. Board members know the institution's culture and with a well-chosen word or action may keep a new president from wandering or being led into trouble. Does the president's house or office require remodeling? The job should have been done, in quiet consultation with the next residents, well before the new president arrives. If renovation must go forward now, it may need to be done more modestly and paid for over several budget years. Is the president preparing to dismiss long-serving (and possibly much beloved) staff? Consider advising that such major moves be put off a while until he or she is better established. Are plans for an inauguration too lavish? Are commitments outpacing resources and planning? Is early rhetoric too grandiose? Are key donors or political supporters being neglected? If only because many presidents have fallen victim to these excesses and omissions, the board should be prepared to provide warnings and suggest new directions.

To provide additional support through the transition period, boards may want to secure for the new president the services of an independent executive coach. Answering only to the president, a leadership coach can provide professional guidance and counsel with the full assurance that discussions will be held close and not revealed to members of the board to whom the president ultimately reports.

The transition period is also the time to put in place a support structure for the new president's spouse or partner, designed to complement that individual's professional needs, while helping fulfill responsibilities related to the institution. Some boards

---

[43] Theodore J. Marchese, "Making the Most of Presidential Transitions," *Trusteeship*, January/February 2012, p. 29.

ask a member to serve as the spouse or partner's liaison to ease the transition while help-ing to shape the most productive role for the spouse or partner on campus and in the community.

Finally, as mentioned in Chapter 3, another valuable ally of the new president may in some cases be his or her predecessor. But this help should generally come in the form of a few substantive conversations, then a considerate absence from the scene that might stretch over the full three to six months. Ideally the departing president will be happy to be contacted and be helpful when advice is sought but otherwise will allow his or her successor to become established as soon as possible as the institution's only leader.

AN AD HOC TRANSITION GROUP

As explained in Chapter 1, presidential searches should take place within a larger frame-work of transition planning. Ideally, this function is ongoing and already has helped fa-cilitate things at various points. It may be instrumental, for example, in ensuring good communication with the previous president about his or her plans for departure, pro-viding guidance on the composition of the search committee and the search firms to be interviewed, and offering personal hosts to finalists' families during the on-campus interviews so that the latter could be introduced to the resources in the community. The board is always responsible for seeing that the function of transition planning is attended to.

The kind of hands-on transition work that happens post-appointment is often delegated and ad hoc. It is not so much handled directly by the executive committee or a standing committee of the board as by a wider, more representative group (formed by the board) to ease the new president's entry as the search approaches its conclusion. At their best, transition groups help presidents-elect understand campus culture and serve as sounding boards and occasionally counselors for new leaders.

One or more board members (perhaps ideally ones who have served on the search committee) do need to be appointed to this group and report back on its activities. But its membership should probably include representatives of the faculty, staff, student body, and possibly alumni and community.

On-Campus Support and Activities

Any ad hoc transition group might meet with the president—if only by phone—soon after the appointment to introduce itself, clarify its responsibilities, and get his or her thoughts and suggestions. Presidents may, for example, find it helpful for a transition committee to design, distribute, and compile the results of a survey of the community, organize focus groups, or take the lead in arranging introductions to significant campus groups and/or brief visits prior to the move to campus. Such steps can help orient a new president to different constituencies' hopes and concerns and help demonstrate a wish to know the institution and listen carefully to the insights of those who understand it best. The ad hoc group can also assist by highlighting and helping to shape events during the early months that present good opportunities for the president to show interest and support for ongoing work and be welcomed and more widely introduced. Student members may serve as liaisons to student organizations. Board members should help ensure that the president meets all members of the board, either at their homes or businesses or over a meal or in some other social setting. The group may take the lead in structuring a set of early meetings of the president-elect with senior administrators and staff in the president's office. It may want to ensure that the president gets a systematic tour of the institution's physical plant from the staff responsible for each facility.

> **❝ The transition group may want to coordinate a series of retreats involving key administrators, faculty leaders, and members of the governing board. These can serve an important social and trust-building function. ❞**

The transition group may want to coordinate a series of retreats involving key administrators, faculty leaders, and members of the governing board. These can serve an important social and trust-building function and, especially when spaced out over a period of several months, allow for the building of a very serviceable consensus about the institution's situation and the priorities that must be addressed.

External Constituencies

An ad hoc transition group should focus on external constituencies as well, setting up meetings with alumni, donors, business leaders, and business groups (such as Rotary clubs and chambers of commerce). Meetings with system leadership are essential for presidents of public institutions. Meetings with national, state, and local government officials, leaders of public and independent schools, and the leadership of sponsoring religious denominations may be appropriate. The new president should certainly be scheduled to meet with local and regional media. Not every conversation warrants a separate meeting or appointment; receptions, breakfasts, luncheons, and dinners can all provide the kind of occasion needed. What's important is that the president be seen as reaching out, make the acquaintance of those whose support is needed, and—ideally—make a good first impression.[44]

Spouses, Partners, and Families

Other tasks for such a group might include giving special attention to the personal needs of the new president and his or her spouse, partner, or family. Timely help linking them up with appropriate employment opportunities, schools, doctors, and other community resources can prevent the new leader's having to deal with major distractions. Such gestures greatly increase the chances that these newest members of the community will settle happily in.

Key Points

- **In the critical first three to six months of a new president's term, an ad hoc transition group can help the new president learn about the institution**, meet and hear from internal and external constituencies, and in other ways assume his or her leadership responsibilities with growing effectiveness.

- **In a friendly transition, the outgoing president might counsel and assist the successor when requested** but otherwise step aside and mostly stay out of view for a period so that the successor can more easily establish himself or herself as the institution's only leader.

---

[44] Stanley and Betts, "A Proactive Model," pp. 90–92, and Zimpher, "Presidential Turnover," pp. 123–31 in Martin and Samels, *Presidential Transition*.

- **The board works with the president during this period to set clear expectations and metrics** and clarify questions of communications and decision making.

- **Building the working relationship between the board chair and new president deserves special attention** during these early months of a presidency.

Additional Articles from *Trusteeship*

Artman, Richard B. and Mark Franz. "Presidential Transition Teams: Fostering a Collaborative Transition Process." *Trusteeship* pp. (July/August 2009): p. 28.

Fennell, Marylouise and Scott D. Miller. "If Your President Needs a Mentor..." *Trusteeship* (May/June 2005): pp. 25-28.

Kunkel, Thomas. "The Education of a Freshman President." *Trusteeship* (March/April 2010): p. 29.

Riggs, Janet Morgan and Robert Duelks. "The Chair and the New President: Getting the First Months Right," *Trusteeship* (January/February 2012): pp. 30–33.

Thornburgh, John K. "360 Degrees Support for the 24/7 President." *Trusteeship* (March/April 2007): pp. 23.

For more recommended reading, please see Resources at the end of this book.

IN SUMMARY:
Looking Back, Looking Forward

W E BEGAN BY NOTING the importance of presidential selection in the life of the institution. For everyone concerned, the challenge of choosing a new president carries risk, but also enormous opportunity. Here at the end of the process, a look back will probably confirm these facts. It also no doubt reveals something touched on briefly before: What seem to be byproducts of the selection process can turn out to be among its most valuable results.

The analysis of institutional needs on which the criteria for the new president are based can unite board members, faculty, administration, students, alumni, and state educational officers on the mission of the college or university. The intense, sustained collaboration of all those on the search committee fosters mutual understanding and trust and helps point a direction for moving the college or university forward. The manner in which the committee represents and communicates with the many interested constituencies—the media, candidates, nominators, references, students, faculty, staff, alumni, parents, and the local community—says something important about a campus's values, nature, and style. Done correctly, a search—even more than producing new leadership—can begin to renew an institution.

Best practices. How to do a search correctly has of course been this book's topic. The guidance it provides recognizes the many forms the process can take. But it underscores as well the importance of some common elements:

- Transition planning;
- A representative, well-led and well-organized search committee;
- An experienced search consultant;
- Widespread agreement on criteria;
- Aggressive outreach to candidates;
- Thoughtful vetting;
- Productive interviews;
- The right balance of openness and confidentiality;
- Good communication with candidates and the community;
- Well-planned campus visits;
- Persuasive presentation of the opportunity;
- An effective contract negotiation; and
- A well-thought out launch.

We hope this book has added to readers' understanding of the process that these many elements comprise. It's a challenging one in the best of circumstances. But getting it right can advantage a college or university for years to come.

APPENDICES

Appendix A

SAMPLE BOARD'S CHARGE TO THE SEARCH COMMITTEE

[Name of Institution]
Charge to the Presidential Search Committee

The board of trustees of [name of institution] appreciates the presidential search committee's willingness to undertake the important work that will lead to the appointment of the next president of [name of institution]. The following charge and confidentiality statement outlines the board's expectations with respect to the search process, confidentiality expected of the committee and the authority granted to the search committee:

1. The search committee will adopt a timetable for the search that will permit the appointment of a president by [date], or as soon thereafter as possible.

2. The search committee will conduct an active national search to attract highly qualified candidates.

3. The search committee will make periodic reports to members of the [name of institution] community and to the board about the progress of the search.

4. The search committee will observe strict confidentiality in the conduct of the search. Any member of the search committee who breaches confidentiality may be removed from the committee without replacement.

5. The search committee will meet with the board after on-campus interviews with finalists to recount its work and to provide the board with comments regarding strengths and concerns for each of the finalists interviewed.

_____   _____
Search Committee Member   Chair, Presidential Search Committee

_____   _____
Date   Date

Appendix B

SAMPLE SEARCH TIMETABLE

MONTH 1

Plan and Organize the Search

1. Board of trustees appoints and charges search committee
2. Search firm speaks with board and conducts on-campus needs assessment
3. Position profile and advertisement completed and approved by committee
4. Presidential ad placed in *Chronicle of Higher Education*, online and minority-serving publications
5. Active recruitment begins
6. Communicate with campus community

MONTH 2

Recruit a Strong, Diverse, and Inclusive Pool

1. Call for nominations and focused recruitment initiated
2. Screening begins
3. Committee begins to narrow pool
4. Initial short list identified
5. Reference checking completed and shared
6. Transition planning initiated

MONTH 3

Screen and Evaluate Candidate List

1. Committee selects six to eight candidates for confidential interviews
2. Search firm conducts deep reference checks on candidates
3. Confidential, neutral-site interviews conducted
4. Committee selects final candidates for campus interviews
5. Transition plan begins to take shape

MONTH 4

Interview Candidates and Evaluate Committee Recommendations

1. Campus interviews scheduled and hosted
2. Meeting of search committee following campus visits to develop recommendation to the board of trustees
3. Search committee meets with board of trustees to present recommendations
4. Board deliberates and authorizes executive committee to extend offer to leading candidate

MONTH 5

Launch Successfully

1. Transition team organized and charged
2. Transition plan implemented

Appendix C

SAMPLE ESTIMATED SEARCH BUDGET

Consultant fee	$	75,000

Includes clerical, research, and administrative services,
including postage, copies, fax, and phone charges

Travel, food, and lodging (two consultants for four trips)

Consultants (@ $1000 per consultant)	8,000
Candidates (8 semifinalists and 3 finalists @$1000 per candidate)	11,000

Advertising

Online	1,500
Print	5,500

Background checks

Three candidates @ $200	600

Total	$	101,600

(Note: The full cost of a search may include additional institutional expeditures.)

Appendix D

SAMPLE POSITION PROFILE

Public Institution

_____ seeks a new president. This individual must possess high academic and personal standards, be energetic and persistent in the pursuit of excellence, and be comfortable with the values and lifestyle of the university's region. The principal professional qualities sought are:

Academic Leader committed to high-quality undergraduate liberal education and to its value in the disciplines of the liberal arts and sciences and in preprofessional education.

- Broadly familiar with assessment strategies appropriate to liberal education and in particular with the strengths and weaknesses of value-added assessment; and
- Demonstrating in formal education and experience academic standards commensurate with the mission of the university and the goals of its faculty.

Evaluator/Planner committed to rigorous completion of the current five-year plan.

- Able to develop details for its implementation while simultaneously advancing the aims of the plan into the next phase of development;
- Able to establish procedures for a continuous planning process; and
- Able to balance a statewide liberal arts mission with local and regional service needs.

Effective Administrator possessing experience in administration at a high level in an institution at least equal in complexity and scope to _____.

- Able to discriminate between areas where further change should be encouraged and those which require increased stability;
- Willing to work with a campus administration that has purposefully been kept lean in comparison to investment in academic resources;

- Able to guide a gradual redistribution of resources to support services in a manner consistent with the maintenance of core educational goals;
- Sufficiently informed in key administrative areas, particularly budget and admissions;
- Able to balance administrative responsibilities with access for faculty, staff, and students;
- Able to select excellent staff; and
- Able to delegate but be decisive.

Community Developer committed to the development of strong internal and external communities.

- Willing to value and encourage widespread understanding for and participation in major decisions affecting the university;
- Able to build bridges between external and internal communities; and
- Particularly effective in interpreting the academic mission of the university, including the importance of assessment and its value in liberal education, to its various constituencies.

Resource Acquirer demonstrating by prior experience the personal and professional skills necessary to represent the university and its mission to the state of [name of state].

- Adept at creating and presenting the university's budgetary program; and
- Knowledgeable about funding possibilities in the private sector.

Appendix D continued

SAMPLE POSITION PROFILE

Independent Institution

_____ College offers quality, affordable undergraduate and graduate education that emphasizes both career education and the liberal arts. It has an enrollment of [number] full-time students and [number] part-time students in the evening and continuing education programs. The entering scores of students have progressed steadily in recent years. The college is debt-free and has a modern, well-maintained physical plant. Its endowment of $X million is equal to its annual operating budget, and the college has never suffered an annual operating deficit.

The next president of _____College must possess integrity and high energy, should preferably have an earned doctorate, and demonstrate the following attributes:

Academic

The president must understand the nature and purpose of undergraduate and graduate education. In particular, the individual must respect the qualities of good teaching and their application both to professional and liberal arts courses. He or she should be able to lead the college in a thorough review of its core curriculum. The president should assist the institution in establishing an effective balance between programs that generate enrollments and those necessary to maintain curricular integrity.

Management

The president must demonstrate the ability to manage an enterprise at least equal in complexity to that of _____ College. He or she must be particularly skilled in fiscal management. On the whole, the board favors the continuation of the policy of fiscal conservatism that has served the college well for 35 years. At the same time, the new president will also be expected to use the college's current and expected future financial health to develop and encourage new educational ventures. Finally, the individual should be open to developing responsible participation of faculty and staff in the decision process.

Planning

_____ College has gone through a decade of enrollment and physical growth. Some additional building will be necessary, but it must be carefully selected and be related to the fulfillment of specific program obligations in selected academic areas and student support services. The next president must understand planning and apply it in the creation of a comprehensive plan that recognizes existing commitments and identifies new opportunities. The president should be able to articulate a vision of the college's future and to involve the college community in its attainment.

Community Relations

_____ College draws its students from all parts of [name of region], but it still retains a strong and special relation to the [specific location community]. The president should be willing to be involved in that community. Such involvement should be an integral part of his or her past experience. The president should value the 12,000 alumni as a special element among its constituents and lead the college in even greater involvement of the alumni with its future.

Human Relations

_____ College benefits from an informal, friendly campus atmosphere. Faculty are closely involved with students. The president must be comfortable with a high degree of personal interaction with the campus and all its constituent groups—faculty, students, and staff. The president should encourage high standards and high performance from all members of the campus community, creating incentives and encouragement that help produce those results.

Resource Development

The president should demonstrate knowledge of and, preferably, substantial prior experience with fund-raising and resource acquisition. For its future health, _____ College will rely on a combination of strong financial management of current operations, cultivation of local resources, and the development of a larger base of donors, including alumni. The president will be expected to provide leadership and direction in this area and should consider it an area requiring a high degree of personal involvement.

Appendix E

SAMPLE LIST OF MATERIALS FOR CANDIDATES

Applicants and Nominees

Catalogue (or link to online version)

Admissions viewbook (or link to online version)

Position profile

Summary of institutional characteristics

Semifinalists

President's report for the last three years

Executive summary from the latest accreditation report

Specialized program brochures

Institutional research studies

Long-term planning documents

Faculty and staff handbook

Finalists

Budgets and audit reports (current and past two years)

Fundraising history (three years, projected and actual)

Enrollment history (three years, projected and actual)

Minutes of major board meetings

Self-studies and consultants' reports

Senior and alumni surveys

Appendix F

SAMPLE CANDIDATE RATING FORM

Candidate_____

Current Position_____

Current Institution_____

Degree and Field_____

Previous Positions/Institutions_____

_____

DESIRED PRESIDENTIAL ATTRIBUTES

1 – Superior **2** – Above Average **3** – Average **4** – Below Average **5** – Unknown

Attributes	Evaluation					Comments
	1	2	3	4	5	
Leadership – Progression of Leadership Experiences						
Accomplishment – Success in Previous Assignments						
Fundraising – Aptitude/ Experience						
Community Relations/ Partnerships						
Strategic Planning – Knowledge/Experience						

Attributes	Evaluation					Comments
	1	2	3	4	5	
Knowledge/Experience with Shared Governance Model						
Communication Skills – Written, Verbal, Listening						
Financial and Budget Acumen						
Commitment to Mission of Institution						
Student Focus						
Global Perspective						
Experience as Team Player/Team Builder						

Overall impressions from the resume and letter:

_____

_____

_____

Should we advance this candidate to the finalist stage?

___ Yes   ___ Maybe   ___ No

Resources

Atwell, Robert. *Presidential Compensation in Higher Education: A Guide for Governing Boards.* Washington, DC: Association of Governing Boards of Universities and Colleges, 2008.

Center for Policy Analysis. *The American College President 2012*. Washington, DC: American Council on Education, 2012.

Dowdall, Jean A. *Searching for Higher Education Leadership: Advice for Candidates and Search Committees.* Lanham, MD: Rowman and Littlefield, 2007.

Martin, James, James E. Samels, and Associates. *Presidential Transition in Higher Education: Managing Leadership Change.* Baltimore: Johns Hopkins University Press, 2004.

Morrill, Richard L. *Assessing Presidential Effectiveness: A Guide for College and University Boards.* Washington, DC: Association of Governing Boards of Universities and Colleges, 2010.

Presidential Search: An Overview for Board Members. Washington, DC: Association of Governing Boards of Universities and Colleges, 2012.

Tebbe, Don. *Chief Executive Transitions: How to Hire and Support a Nonprofit CEO.* Washington, DC: BoardSource, 2008.

Additional resources are available at *www.agb.org*.

ABOUT THE AUTHORS

Joseph S. Johnston, Jr., is senior consultant for administration for AGB Search, a national consulting firm that assists colleges and universities in planning for, recruiting, selecting, and transitioning new executive leaders.

For more than three decades, he has served in a variety of positions in higher education: lecturer in English and assistant to two presidents at Bryn Mawr College, research associate with the Institute for Research on Higher Education at the University of Pennsylvania, vice president for programs and vice president for education and global initiatives at the Association of American Colleges and Universities, and senior vice president at The Washington Center.

Johnston is the author or co-author of numerous publications related to higher education, including several books on the integration of liberal and professional education and one on international education. He has consulted widely to colleges and universities. He has also served on a number of governing and advisory boards, including those of the National Humanities Alliance, National Security Education Program, University of North Carolina—Asheville, and Warren Wilson College.

A native of Virginia, Joe Johnston graduated with Phi Beta Kappa honors from Randolph-Macon College. He holds an M.B.A. in finance from the Wharton School of the University of Pennsylvania and a Ph.D. in English literature from the University of Chicago.

James P. Ferrare is senior vice president of the Association of Governing Boards of Universities and Colleges and principal of its affiliate AGB Search. Before joining AGB, Ferrare was a past president and senior consultant with Academic Search, Inc., where he served for 10 years, completing more than 80 searches. He has led searches for presidents, academic vice presidents, and deans in public and private colleges and universities as well as church-affiliated schools and independent liberal arts and fine arts institutions.

Prior to joining Academic Search, he was dean of the school of education at Drake University. As dean, he enacted many of the very lessons he taught in his faculty role as associate professor of leadership and adult development. He also led a string of successful searches for university administrators, faculty members, and high-profile school superintendents. Prior to his deanship, Ferrare was a faculty member and assistant dean responsible for policy development, budgeting, and student support.

Before coming to Drake, he served as associate executive director of the school administrators of Iowa and as associate superintendent of schools for the nationally renowned West Des Moines Community School district. He also has taught elementary and middle school.

Ferrare earned his B.S. in education and his M.Ed. in reading and education from the Edinboro University of Pennsylvania. He holds a Ph.D. in educational administration from Iowa State University.

About AGB's Mission:

In today's environment, knowledgeable, committed, and engaged boards are central to the success of colleges and universities. AGB helps board members and college and university leaders address governance and leadership challenges by providing vital information, fostering effective collaboration, building board capacity, and serving as a trusted advisor. Our programs, publications, meetings, and services offer a range of ways to improve board governance and institution leadership.

Who are AGB Members?

AGB counts the boards of over 1,250 colleges, universities, and institutionally related foundations among its members. Boards join AGB to provide resources for exceptional governance to board members and senior staff. The 36,000 individual board members and institutional leaders AGB serves come from colleges and universities of all types (independent and public, four-year and two-year, general and specialized) as well as foundations affiliated with public universities.

How Can You Engage?

AGB membership extends to every individual member of the board and selected members of the institution's administration. By virtue of their institution's membership in AGB, individuals receive access to all of AGB's services, knowledge, and real-time solutions to pressing governance and leadership issues.

AGB members become more engaged in their roles; they gain access to vital information, benefit from the expertise of our skilled staff and consultants, and are better able to support their institution's application of key principles and practices of higher education governance. Explore the benefits of AGB membership and further support your institution's mission. Start by visiting *www.agb.org*.

AGB has many members-only resources online. For log-in information and password access, visit *www.agb.org* or contact: *dpd@agb.org*